SURROUNDING
YOURSELF WITH THE
RIGHT PEOPLE

SURROUNDING
YOURSELF WITH THE
RIGHT PEOPLE

HOW YOUR FRIENDS AND ASSOCIATIONS
INFLUENCE YOUR SUCCESS

DR. DENNIS SEMPEBWA

DESTINY IMAGE™ EUROPE srl
Via Maiella, 1
66020 San Giovanni Teatino (Ch) – Italy

"Changing the world, one book at a time."

This book and all other Destiny Image™ Europe books are available at Christian bookstores and distributors worldwide.

To order products, or for any other correspondence:

DESTINY IMAGE™ EUROPE srl
Via Acquacorrente, 6
65123 - Pescara - Italy
Tel. +39 085 4716623 - Fax: +39 085 9431270
E-mail: info@eurodestinyimage.com
Or reach us on the Internet: www.eurodestinyimage.com

ISBN: 978-88-96727-00-3
For Worldwide Distribution, Printed in the U.S.A.
1 2 3 4 5 6 7 8 / 14 13 12 11 10

DEDICATION

This book is dedicated to all the godly relationships I have been privileged to enjoy. Thank you for allowing me to share your journey!

Acknowledgments

To my precious wife and number one Cheerleader, Ingrid. You, my love, are invaluable to me. Thank you for loving me through it all.

To our lovely chocolates, Adam, Abigail, Caleb, and Judah. You all teach me so much. I am so honored that you call me Daddy.

My incredible mother, Deborah Sempebwa, for my first lessons in relationship management; and my brothers, Duncan and Dixon, and sisters, Sylvia, Samallie, and Susan—I love you all.

My mentors, Dr. Myles Munroe and Dr. David Sumrall, for allowing me to closely observe your walk of faith. I appreciate you more than words can express.

Pietro Evangelista, thank you for believing in this work and for waiting three years to publish it. I am looking forward to an amazing journey with you and the entire Destiny Image Europe team.

Bill Vander Velde, for your part in making this dream a reality. Godspeed, my friend!

To Mzee Phillip Myles. Thank you—words cannot express my appreciation to you.

To Pastor John Nordstrom. Ingrid and I cannot thank you enough for walking with us through our darkest moments. Your impact has opened a new world to me. I will be forever grateful.

To the entire ministry team and church family of Sanctuary of Life. What an honor it has been to walk with you all! I am looking forward to growing together.

To all my Cheerleaders, thank you for laughing with me, crying with me, dreaming with me, and walking with me.

To all my Coaches, thank you for showing me your scars and allowing me to sit by your feet and learn from your journeys.

Finally, to the Conduits in my life. It's been an honor and a privilege pouring into your lives.

Endorsements

Surrounding Yourself With the Right People is indispensable reading for anyone who wants to live life above the norm. It is one of the most profound, practical, principle-centered approaches to this subject of relationships I have read in a long time. This is a profound authoritative work that spans the wisdom of the ages, and yet breaks new ground in its approach. It will possibly become a classic in this and the next generation. This book is destined to be a required reading for all who want to succeed in life—a must for the progressive mind.

Dr. Myles Munroe, Senior Pastor
Founder, Bahamas Faith Ministries International
Nassau, Bahamas

The world can be a lonely place for so many, often due to hurts from wrong or superficial relationships. Dr. Dennis Sempebwa brings practical and profound wisdom with insight from his own experiences. He tackles this necessary subject, giving the reader essential ingredients for healthy relationships so he or she can avoid spending time and energy on the wrong ones. Putting the wisdom of this book into practice is vital for building new relationships while maximizing the ones you currently have.

Hank Kunneman, Senior Pastor
Lord of Hosts Church/One Voice Ministries
Omaha, Nebraska, USA

The whole of life can be summed up as a journey of relationships. Relationships, therefore, hold the key to our happiness and growth. Dr. Dennis offers not only knowledge, but also personal experiences and insights into this very important, and at times perilous, journey of relationship building. This book serves as a beacon of hope and light showing the way relationships can work for the good of everyone. A book for all who want their relationships to not be painful or unfulfilling, but rather enjoyable and beneficial.

Daniel and Deborah Cheah, Senior Pastors
His Sanctuary of Glory Church/HSG Global Ministries
Kuala Lumpur, Malaysia

The longer I live and the older I get, the more I realize that life is *all* about relationships, period! Nothing else comes even close. And as a pastor, I've had plenty of opportunities to observe the good, bad, and ugly of that principle. My friend, Dennis, has done us all a favor by bringing this principle to life in the pages of this book. Don't read it just for its colorful stories of his experiences from childhood in Uganda to ministry around the globe—read it to apply its truths to your own life while there's still time, because it's never too late to heal a relationship from the past, or to forge a new friendship that will bless your future. Thanks, Dennis, for showing us the way!

Jerry McQuay, Senior Pastor
Christian Life Center
Tinley Park, Illinois, USA

Dr. Sempebwa lays out a brilliant blueprint for anyone who desires to be successful. The old adage "Birds of a feather flock together" is skillfully outlaid in this book. Anyone desiring to become successful and stay successful will surround him or herself with an all-star team. Dennis gives timeless principles in assembling this team. This book is a must-read.

Dr. Will Moreland, Senior Pastor
International Gospel Church
Kitzingen, Germany

Of all the treasures in the world, nothing compares to the riches of a true friend. Conversely, nothing hurts more than the sting of a friendship in ruins. Relationships will either drive us to greatness or drain us. In this book, Dennis reveals the practical recipe for uncovering the treasures of true friendship and recovering from the pain of broken ones. You will cherish the relevant message of his book as it helps you heal and equips you to develop life-changing relationships.

Scott Holmes, Senior Pastor
Life Church
Shreveport, Louisiana, USA

Dr. Sempebwa sure knows what it takes to keep the covenant and commitments of a relationship, and that qualifies him to write this insightful book.

Clemet Ibe, Senior Pastor
Bethesda Christian Center
Pretoria, South Africa

A Spanish proverb says: "Tell me who you hang around with, and I will tell you who you are, for he who hangs around with wolves will learn to howl." Many have made the terrible mistake of neglecting this vital subject of relationships. This very revealing book identifies vital tools needed to engage in any kind of relationship. For those desiring effective relationships, this book is a must-read.

Luis A. Morales, Senior Pastor
Vida Real Evangelical Center
Somerville, Massachusetts, USA

Occasionally I find a book that makes me think that a subject could not be better explored; this is such a book. In this brilliant work, Dr. Dennis has distilled the best principles in understanding the vast, complex world of relationships. I have no doubt that this book will be a favorite on the subject the world over.

Lincoln Serwanga, Senior Pastor
Liberty Christian Fellowship
London, UK

As a minister of the Good News, Dr. Dennis Sempebwa rightly imparts the Word. He sounds the trumpet and informs us that there is a balm in Gilead and bread at the walls of Jerusalem. Dennis is a friend who likes to add value to his friends, and through his book he will enrich your life. I have every confidence this book will prove an indispensable tool to everyone who wants to increase their effectiveness in God's Kingdom through right relationships.

Dr. Buni Cocar, Author, Evangelist
Senior Pastor, Maranatha Church
Chicago, Illinois, USA

TABLE OF CONTENTS

FOREWORD

Show me your friends, and I will show you your future. These words are true and must be considered on your journey through life. This is the heart of *Surrounding Yourself With the Right People*.

This erudite, eloquent, and immensely thought-provoking work gets to the heart of the deepest passions and aspirations of the human heart as it relates to the priority, value, and necessity of the right relationships in our lives.

Surrounding Yourself With the Right People is indispensable reading for anyone who wants to live life above the norm. This is a profound, authoritative work that spans the wisdom of the ages and yet breaks new ground in its approach. It will possibly become a classic in this and the next generation.

This exceptional work by Dennis Sempebwa is one of the most profound, practical, principle-centered approaches to the subject of relationships I have read in a long time. The author's approach to this timely issue brings a fresh breath of air that captivates the heart, engages the mind, and inspires the spirit of the reader to consider all those we allow in our circle of influence.

The author's ability to leap over complicated theological and metaphysical jargon and reduce complex theories to simple, practical principles that the least among us can understand is amazing.

This work will challenge the intellectual while embracing the layperson as it dismantles the mysteriousness of the soul search of humankind and delivers the profound in simplicity.

Dennis's approach awakens in the reader the untapped inhibiters that retard our personal development through relationships, and his antidotes empower us to rise above these self-defeating, self-limiting factors to a life of exploits in spiritual and mental advancement and personal success.

The author also integrates into each chapter the time-tested precepts, giving each principle a practical application to life, making the entire process people-friendly.

Every sentence of this exciting book is pregnant with wisdom, and I enjoyed the mind-expanding experience. I admonish you to plunge into this ocean of knowledge and watch your life change for the better.

Dr. Myles Munroe
Founder, Bahamas Faith Ministries International
International Third World Leaders Association
Nassau, Bahamas

PREFACE

I was born and raised in the East African nation of Uganda. At the time, we were the thirteenth poorest country in the world. The country was filled with unimaginable political turmoil and a decrepit economic base. It was rare to have more than one meal a day. Consequently, we had to improvise—make do.

Every morning, I made it a point to walk through a mango farm on my way to school. There I would pick my breakfast—juicy Ugandan mangoes. After tasting various species from different parts of the world, I am persuaded that none compare to these delicious Ugandan mangoes!

After filling my little tummy with as many as I could possibly eat, I stuffed one or two mangoes into my pockets to eat during recess. As soon as the bell rang, I would run to the farthest corner of our school playground to savor my mango uninterrupted. I loved my peaceful routine.

But once in awhile, though, I would bite into a mango, only to quickly spit it out. It was rotten. Yikes! What a disappointment.

Relationships can cause the same disappointment. While walking through life we pick people, befriend them, and intimate with them. Like mangoes, they look, smell, and feel right when we pick them. It is not until we have walked a certain distance or through certain circumstances with them that we know their true state.

At some time or another, we have all picked unripe or rotten mangoes—and people. In fact, I like to say it this way: if you have never picked a bad mango, you have never been mango picking! Likewise, if you have loved with your heart, you have been hurt because none of us are perfect. We have all experienced hurtful relationships and carry scars from wrong associations. Unfortunately, it is through the prism of these scars that we view current and future relationships.

This book is about relationships and how to surround yourself with the right people who will provide benefits for both of you. I do not claim to be a relationship expert; my "expertise" comes from real-life experiences, both good and bad. Like you, I have been loved by wonderful people, but I have also been hurt by people whom I loved and trusted. From these experiences, I have learned a lot, and I share proven, successful principles that will help you overcome past pain and move forward into healthy relationships.

As I listen to some of the greatest men and women in Christendom today, and as I peruse the memoirs of yesterday's generals, at the end of many a rich life, they all seem to say the same thing: "If I were to do this over again, I would invest more time and effort in right relationships. I would not waste irredeemable time trying to please the wrong people. I would pour my life into those who were genuinely interested in my future. I would love my spouse more, play longer with my kids, and be available to my friends. I'm sorry that I did not maximize my relationships—surround myself with the right people." From this wisdom I decided to dedicate the past five years studying this important, life-changing subject.

∽

I have had the honor of serving God as a young drummer, choral singer, church keyboard player, worship director, youth minister, evangelist, recording artist, academician, author, global speaker, and pastor. I believe that, more than ever, we need relational healing. Regardless what you do or where you serve, everyone yearns for and desires enriching relationships.

It is my prayer that this book equips you with the tools you need to maximize your relationships and moves you toward fulfilling your God-given destiny.

May the Holy Spirit cause illumination as you journey through the pages.

RELATIONSHIPS — GOD'S IDEA

No road is long with good company.
—Turkish Proverb

The following stories exemplify relationships gone awry, and are versions of circumstances that many people face. No one is immune to broken relationships—but knowing how to handle these issues empowers you to take the steps necessary to keep moving forward in life.

THE MISSIONARY KID

"Pastor, we have a huge problem," laments Jenny. "We desperately need your counsel. Ken is in big trouble!"

John and Jenny are missionaries in Thailand. They return home every six months for fellowship and fundraising with local churches in their hometown in the suburbs of Atlanta. While their only son, Ken, is out with his buddies, they had the great idea to clean up his room as a surprise. It would give them time to chat about their next trip back to the mission field.

An hour into "operation clean-up," John received a call from his field supervisor asking if he had reviewed the financial report yet. His immediate input was needed to finalize preparations for the annual board meeting and partner dinner the following day.

Instead of driving downtown to his office, John decides to use Ken's computer to download the report. A slight move of the mouse reveals the picture of a nude woman. John fumbles to close the image, only to realize that there are pages and pages of explicit sexual material plastered all over the screen. John's shock is temporarily masked by his haste to close the offensive pages before Jenny sees them. Unfortunately, he is too late. She is completely devastated.

"We are shocked, hurt, and extremely disappointed," says John. "We raised this kid on the mission field. How did he get sucked into this dark world? What do we do? Recently, he has been real secretive. We feel that confronting him with this will only push him farther away from us. How do we handle this delicate situation without losing our only child forever?"

UNFAITHFUL LUCY

Joe is the president and CEO of a very large software company. One Friday morning he instructs his secretary to cancel all his appointments, and instead make lunch reservations for him and his wife, Lucy, at their favorite Italian restaurant downtown. *Lucy just hasn't been herself lately. Something must be up. Perhaps this impromptu lunch together will cheer her up and give us some time to reconnect*, he thinks.

Friday is Lucy's "play day." After a good long workout, she likes to go to the hair salon with her friends and then lunch at her favorite café. Joe decides to meet her at the gym with a lovely bouquet of peonies, her favorite flower. Tina, the receptionist, knows Joe and is more than happy to find her for him. "She walked into the lady's locker room awhile ago," says Tina. "I will be glad to find her for you, Joe. I can't wait to see her face when she sees those beautiful flowers!"

After what seems like forever, Tina emerges with some not-so-good news. "Joe, I can't find Lucy anywhere. I even checked up in the work-out area. She must have slipped out. Sorry."

"Thanks for looking. I'll find her," Joe declares with resignation. As he steps outside the gym, he notices Lucy's car. *Aha, that explains it*, he thinks. *She is in her mobile office, counseling with one of her girl-friends as usual.*

As Joe approaches the car, he notices that Lucy is not alone. He wonders whether he should interrupt or not, but decides that she will proba-bly be flattered by his flowerful, romantic intrusion. *I'll sneak up from the back and flush the peonies in front of her side of the window. This gab session will immediately be over when she sees the flowers!*

Then Joe notices that Peter, his vice president, is in the passenger's seat. *Those two are always up to something,* he reasons. *They must be planning some office event or the annual staff appreciation party next month. That's even more reason to barge in on them. This is her day off—work can wait until tomorrow.*

As he approaches her window, he notices her hand stroking Peter's thigh, and he is running his hand though her hair and rubbing her shoulder. Joe freezes. *I must be dreaming. This is not happening.*

For what seems like an eternity, he stands motionless, trying to make sense of it all. Then he retreats to his car, tears welling up in his eyes. He drives to a nearby shopping mall parking lot and for three hours sobs uncontrollably. He is devastated.

Finally he gathers the courage to answer Tina's relentless phone calls. "Lucy is looking for you, sir," she says. "She says she pulled in as you drove away from the gym parking lot. She was at the salon with her friend Mary."

He is disgusted. *Lies, lies, and more lies…how much of our life has been a lie? What do I do now? How do I deal with this without losing the most valuable relationship in my life,* he wonders as he sobs even more.

Betrayed Michael

Michael, a successful pastor of a major non-denominational church, receives a copy of a very disturbing e-mail. It's a memo from his senior associate minister, Jack:

> *Well guys, don't forget our meeting tomorrow night at Charlie's. This will be our final meeting. The day has finally come! By the time Michael wakes up, we will be well into the first phase of our move. Again, please don't be late. AND BE EXTRA CAREFUL…*

It is clear that Michael was inadvertently included in the mailer. Initially, he thinks nothing of it. His birthday is coming up, and maybe they are planning some kind of elaborate surprise celebration. But he is unsettled, so he re-reads the e-mail. "By the time Michel wakes up…" Why would Jack put it this way? Deep inside, he knows that this is much more serious than he cares to admit. He is almost sick to his stomach.

For weeks now, Jack has been evasive. He is constantly on the phone with the other pastors, even during weekly leadership meetings. He keeps text-messaging team leaders and seems to be avoiding eye contact with Michael. *Something is very wrong here,* Michael thinks. He has heard countless stories of church splits, and although he does not want to consider it, this smells like one.

Upon further investigation, the truth is revealed. Jack has been planning a breakaway for months. Everything is set up for an eminent split. They have even persuaded some of the biggest donors to migrate with them.

Michael is devastated. He remembers the long hours he personally invested in helping Jack. All those late night calls from his young, pregnant wife, Kristy. The countless times she wanted to throw in the towel and divorce Jack. It's a miracle what God has done in their lives. Now Jack is a respected leader, both in the church and their local community. Michael is proud to call him one of his spiritual sons. *How do I confront Jack without tearing up the church and destroying everything we have built in the past 30 years?* wonders Michael.

MADE FOR RELATIONSHIP

Friend, you and I are made for relationship. We are not designed to walk through life alone.

In my extensive travels worldwide, I have met some of the most incredible men and women of God. I have had the opportunity to interface with exceptional leaders, business tycoons, and some really amazing achievers. I have also wept with under-privileged people and spent time with outcasts of this world. Because of all these experiences, I have come to this conclusion: the number one struggle for many of us, irrespective of our societal pedigree, is not financial hardships, persecution, or even excessive adversity—the struggle is with our relationships.

There are answers to this struggle—and that is why I wrote this book, to share the answers with you, to help you live victoriously regardless of past or current broken relationships.

I have heard many a well-meaning Christian say, "Dennis, all I need is Jesus. I don't care about other people. Jesus is all I need." Well, that no doubt sounds great and very spiritual, and I can understand why some Christians feel that way, but those types of statements are simply not true.

People need one another. We need relationships with others. There is no such thing as solo-Christianity! We are created for connection, for interdependency. God has ordained that you and I should walk with others. Let's go through the creation story as we examine this important principle.

The Bible says:

> *Then God said, "Let there be light," and there was light. And* **God saw that it was good** (Genesis 1:3-4a).

In Genesis 1:10, we read:

> *God named the dry ground "land" and the water "seas." And* **God saw that it was good.**

God proceeds to create seed-bearing plants, trees, fruits, and diverse species of flora. Again, He is so pleased with His handiwork that the Bible says:

> *And* **God saw that it was good** (Genesis 1:12b).

God then creates the sun, moon, and stars, setting them in their places and ordaining their functions. At the end of an undoubtedly rewarding fourth day, the Bible tells us that:

> *And* **God saw that it was good** (Genesis 1:18b).

On day five, God focuses on inhabiting the sea and air. We read:

> *So God created great sea creatures and every sort of fish and every kind of bird. And* **God saw that it was good** (Genesis 1:21).

On the sixth day, the Bible says that:

> *God made all sorts of wild animals, livestock, and small animals, each able to reproduce more of its own kind. And* **God saw that it was good** (Genesis 1:25).

Then God creates people, patterning them after Himself. He could not be more proud of His handiwork—His creation. The Bible tells us that:

*Then God saw everything that He had made, and **indeed it was very good**...* (Genesis 1:31 NKJV).

The New Living Translation says:

*Then God looked over all He had made, and He saw that **it was excellent in every way**.*

Genesis chapter 2 begins with:

So the creation of the heavens and the earth and everything in them was completed. On the seventh day, having finished His task, God rested from all His work (Genesis 2:1-2).

Clearly, God was on a roll. I can only imagine the jubilation in Heaven as creation after creation was placed within His unique world. After He formed man, God breathed life into him and created a magnificent habitation for him called the Garden of Eden.

*We don't know how long it took God to notice that something was not well with His handiwork. Was it after that last day? And how long was that day? Peter writes, "But you must not forget, dear friends that **a day** is like **a thousand years** to the Lord, and a thousand years is like **a day**"* (2 Peter 3:8).

The Greek word for *thousand* is the word, *chilioi*, which simply means: "plural of uncertain affinity." The Bible uses *a thousand* to depict different enumerations under various circumstances.

For example, the psalmist says:

*For all the animals of the forest are mine, and I own the cattle on **a thousand** hills* (Psalm 50:10).

Clearly, God is not talking about a literal number of hills. He is simply painting a picture of abundance.

The psalmist also writes:

*For a day in thy courts is better than **a thousand**. I had rather be a doorkeeper in the house of my God, than to dwell in the tents of wickedness* (Psalm 84:10 NKJV).

*For You **a thousand** years are as yesterday! Like a few hours!* (Psalm 90:4)

> *Though **a thousand** fall at your side, though ten thousand are dying around you, these evils will not touch you* (Psalm 91:7).

I am sure that you understand. We don't know if the days described in the creation account are the same as our 24-hour days. But regardless of the length of time it took to actually create the heavens and earth with everything them, including Adam, you can imagine the shock when God declares:

> **God said, "It's not good** *for the man to be alone; I'll make him a helper, a companion"* (Genesis 2:18 TM).

In other words, this amazing creation—God's grand finale—man, is not quite perfect. Something is missing. He needs someone with whom to laugh, dance, celebrate, and share life. Man needs relationship.

We can only imagine the level of intimacy that Adam shared with His heavenly Father, Jehovah God Himself. In his sinless state, he openly conversed with God. With no consideration for time as we know it, they must have fellowshipped for hours on end. Can you imagine that type of closeness and intimacy? But even then, God Himself noticed a void in Adam's perfect existence—human relationship!

So God goes on a quest to find a companion for Adam. The Bible says that:

> *...He brought them to Adam to see what he would call them, and Adam chose a name for each one. He gave names to all the livestock, birds, and wild animals...* (Genesis 2:19-20a).

God brings these beautiful creatures to Adam. But not one bird or animal could fill the void man felt for human connectedness. Verse 20 concludes:

> *But still there was no helper just right for him* (Genesis 2:20b).

So what did God do? Let's continue on to the next verse.

> *So the Lord God caused the man to fall into a deep sleep. While the man slept, the Lord God took out one of the man's ribs and closed up the opening. Then the Lord God made a woman from the rib, and He brought her to the man* (Genesis 2:21-22).

God created another "one," just like Adam. In fact, as soon as Adam saw his magnificent companion, he exclaims:

"At last!" the man exclaimed. "This one is bone from my bone, and flesh from my flesh!" (Genesis 2:23)

God knew that Adam needed a companion who was like him—and in the image of Father God. He created a woman who would be a helper, someone who could relate to him on the same level of understanding. It was God's idea to provide man a companion with whom he could share relationship.

VERTICAL AND HORIZONTAL RELATIONSHIPS

Not every relationship serves the same purpose. In this book, I categorize all relationships into two dimensions—vertical relationships and horizontal relationships.

Vertical Relationships deal with how we relate with those above and under us. At various times in our lives, God brings people who guide us through the different seasons of our journey. They include our parents, teachers, guides, mentors, instructors, and coaches. These people are interested in where we are going, in what we must become. I call these people Coaches. On the other side of the vertical continuum are those God brings to us so we can lead and help them navigate through life's treacherous waters. Part of their future seems to be hidden in our attention to their journey. These people include our children, students, protégés, disciples, and apprentices. I call these people Conduits. Hence, there are two types of people within vertical relationships—Coaches and Conduits.

Horizontal Relationships, on the other hand, consist of those people who walk alongside us. These people include our spouses, friends, companions, buddies, mates, pals, and associates. I call these people Companions. On the other side of the horizontal continuum are those whom I believe satan sends into our lives to disrupt and destroy us. I call those Corruptors. This is where we are going to begin our discourse—an in-depth look at Horizontal Relationships.

SECTION I

Horizontal Relationships

*A wise man associating with the vicious becomes an idiot;
a dog traveling with good men becomes a rational being.*
–Arabic Proverb

Chapter One

CORRUPTORS — THOSE
WHO DESTROY

Lie down with dogs, wake up with fleas.
　　　　　　　　　　　　　　　　–French Proverb

My little tummy protests violently. *Yikes, how I did miss that,* I wondered. Suddenly it seems obvious that the mango is bad. I wish I had looked more closely before picking it. I rebuke myself, *Dennis, you need to take time to make sure all the mangoes you pick are good. Smell them, press into them, and even shake them.*

But even as a little boy I realized that no matter what I did, I could not guarantee total avoidance of bad mangoes because this particular species of green mangoes was unique. It was impossible to tell the ripeness, or lack thereof, of the mango by merely looking at it. The surest test was a bite. Until I sank my teeth into it, I could not tell for sure whether it was good or bad.

The same is true for relationships. You may think you have chosen wisely, taken the time to get to know a person, asked relevant questions, and talked about important topics, but sometimes that isn't enough.

The Bible says:

> *There are "friends" who destroy each other, but a real friend sticks closer than a brother* (Proverbs 18:24).

The word *friends* is the Hebrew word *rea*, which means "companion, associate, or one who walks through life with another." This verse in Proverbs clearly tells us that there are two kinds of friends—those who destroy and those who encourage. Let's talk about those who destroy first. I call them Corruptors.

CORRUPTORS

To corrupt means "to taint, to stain, to infect, to mar, to spoil, or cause to decay or make putrid." Another definition is "to alter and destroy the integrity of and cause to be dishonest."

Everyone has had Corruptors in their lives at one time or another. Although they walk alongside you, they have their own agenda and don't really have your best interests in mind.

~

Amelia's boss is an influential government official. Her position as his assistant often allows her access to important meetings and to the "movers and shakers" within the agency. One day Tom, a young, handsome intern, asked Amelia out for lunch. They had a wonderful time and Amelia was thrilled when he called her that evening to set up a dinner date. After a few months of dating, Amelia knew she was falling in love with Tom. He was so attentive, always asking about her work, volunteering to help her with projects, and often dropping by the office to see her.

Amelia finally got up the nerve to start a conversation with Tom about their future together. "What future? We're just friends," he said. The following week, Amelia's boss was escorted out of his office, with vague charges pending against him. Through the office grapevine Amelia heard that Tom had spread rumors about her boss based on something she told him in strict confidence. Amelia is devastated.

THERE IS NO SUCH THING AS A NEUTRAL FRIEND.

At any given time, you are walking with people who add to you, or people who take from you—Corruptors. It is vital to remember that your friends will either stretch or stunt your growth.

The Bible says:

> *He who walks [as a companion] with wise men is wise, but he who associates with [self-confident] fools is [a fool himself and] shall smart for it* (Proverbs 13:20 AMP).

He who walks with wise men will be wise, But the companion of fools will be destroyed (Proverbs 13:20).

In other words, when you associate with productive people, your life will blossom. Walk with wise people, and you will become wise. Conversely, hang out with time wasters or manipulators—Corruptors—and soon your life will be less than successful and even destroyed.

Again, the Bible doesn't say that a fool who associates with fools will be destroyed, but *anyone* who associates with them will be destroyed. Isn't that interesting?

Now here is what fascinates me even more. A fool who decides to change his companions and begins to associate with the wise people becomes wise. On the flip side, a wise man who picks wrong associations and hangs out with fools becomes just like them—a fool.

King David wrote:

Blessed is the man who does not walk in the counsel of the wicked or stand in the way of sinners or sit in the seat of mockers. But his delight is in the law of the Lord, and on His law he meditates day and night. He is like a tree planted by streams of water, which yields its fruit in season and whose leaf does not wither. Whatever he does prospers (Psalm 1:1-3 NIV).

I find the sequence in this Scripture rather remarkable. Here is a godly man who refuses to walk with Corruptors. He does not stand with them or sit with them. Rather, he meditates on God's Word day and night. It is to that man that God promises increase and prosperity. Whatever he does prospers! Wow... what a blessed man!

You Become Like Those Who Surround You.

BAD MANGOES

Take a *good* mango and put it in a bucket full of rotten ones. What happens? It rots. Now take a *bad* mango and place it in a bucket full of good ones. Every time I have done that, the bad mango spoils the bucket full of good mangoes.

Associating with Corruptors will spoil you. These people will stain, infect, mar, spoil, or cause you to compromise your values and even your faith. No doubt you can think of one or more people who have been or are currently part of your life who do not bring out the best in you—people who limit or stymie your potential rather than lifting you up and encouraging you to reach your goals and enjoy all that God has for you.

The Bible advises:

> *Don't befriend angry people or associate with hot-tempered people, or* **you will learn to be like them** *and endanger your soul* (Proverbs 22:24-25).

All of us have fallen into the temptation of thinking that we can somehow influence a close friend to change. But almost every time, the opposite happens. They influence us. They infect us and sway us instead.

Proverbs 22:24-25 clearly tells us one thing: Corruptors are to be avoided. It does not say that they will learn to be like you. On the contrary, you will eventually follow them down the path to destruction—they will destroy you.

Here is how the apostle Paul put it:

> *Do not be so deceived and misled!* **Evil companionships (communion, associations)** *corrupt and deprave good manners and morals and character* (1 Corinthians 15:33 AMP).

NEGATIVE ASSOCIATIONS ARE CONTAGIOUS.

In my book *You Have a Dream*, I write:

> Negative associations are contagious: It is amazing just how many well-meaning Christians violate this principle. They continue to associate or hang out with negative people, hoping to change them in the process. Which is easier, to pull someone up or down? Good rarely influences evil. But evil always influences good.[1]

I hail from the Baganda tribe in Uganda. We are a gracious, largely non-confrontational people. We are a very welcoming people. When early white missionaries and explorers came to Buganda, we embraced them heartily. Together, we championed the spread of Christianity, trade, and industry to the region. They loved us because we did not withstand them, as had most of the other tribes on the continent. They called us, "the graceful, polite, welcoming tribe." Soon though, our strength, which was our warm, pliable nature, became our great weakness when our hospitality was abused. Even so, some of our leaders would not abandon our cultural ethic of non-confrontation. No matter what, the guests in our land would be treated with respect.

As a child I was taught, *"Dennis, when you befriend someone, they are in your life for good. You don't cut people off. That is very rude and unbecoming of a true Muganda (native of the Buganda tribe). You keep friends and walk with them for life!"*

As I began pursuing my dream of living to my full potential, however, I realized the necessity of changing my firmly held cultural belief about lifetime friends. You may be wondering if you can really change your culture. Sure you can, and often should. Please read this startling passage of Scripture with me:

> *...**Don't become so well adjusted to your culture that you fit into it without even thinking.** Instead, fix your attention on God. You'll be changed from the inside out. Readily recognize what he wants from you, and quickly respond to it. **Unlike the culture around you,** always dragging you down to its level of immaturity, God brings the best out of you, develops well-formed maturity in you* (Romans 12:2 TM).

Like all of us I fit into my culture because that's how I was raised and that's how everyone around me thought, acted, and reacted. Consequently, it was "dragging me down to its level of immaturity" as Paul says. Instead of obeying God and running after His will in my life, I was more concerned about pleasing and appeasing my friends. After I accepted Christ as my personal Savior and committed my life to Him, my eyes were opened. I could see Corruptors all around me. I became aware of my need to begin to build positive relationships that would propel me toward my God-given destiny—to fulfilling my dream. My prayer became:

> *God, please bring me people who will add to me; people who will encourage me and really walk with me through this season of my life.*

And indeed He answered me. Though painful and at times very frustrating, I was able to methodically dismantle my cultural mind-set and let God develop what the apostle Paul calls, "well-formed maturity" in me. I began to maximize my friendships, surrounding myself with the right people.

GODLY RELATIONSHIPS PROPEL YOU
TOWARD YOUR DIVINE DESTINY.

QUESTIONS

During this process of building positive relationships, I seriously questioned my cultural beliefs. Of course at times I was tempted to back off and rationalize. *Dennis, aren't you being selfish by looking for friends that add to you? If you cut off your current friends, who will help them? Don't you think it's really arrogant of you to judge them like that? What if someone was considering cutting you off? Wouldn't you want someone to stay friends with you and maybe help you change?*

Questions, questions, questions. Did I receive answers overnight? Certainly not! It was a slow process, and at times, a real struggle. That's why I'm sharing what I learned with you through this book—so you won't have to go through the struggle.

Here is what I realized. Every time I hung out with certain people, I noticed a drain on my spirituality. It was too costly for me to spend time with these friends because I was losing something very precious to me. They had become too expensive. Of course I did not treat them as enemies. In fact, I continued to witness to them, but the intimate friendship we had changed after I realized its exorbitant price.

WHEN FRIENDSHIPS DON'T ADD TO YOUR JOURNEY,
THEY HAVE BECOME TOO EXPENSIVE FOR YOU TO MAINTAIN.

Please read that principle again. *When friendships don't add to your journey, they have become too expensive for you to maintain.* What do I mean? When friendships or associations don't add substance, credibility, and growth into your life, investing additional time and energy into those relationships becomes far too costly.

I determined that my culture was not going to drag me down or hold me back. God began to show me my true friends. Every time I was with these guys, I grew in a variety of positive ways: spiritually, mentally, emotionally, and relationally. I was challenged to pray more, read my Bible more, grow more, and witness to more people. I began to purposely steer away from any former friends who had tagged along with me for years.

I listed all my close associations, asking these rather brutal questions: "Does this person add to me or does he or she take away from me? Does he or she cheer me on or corrupt me?"

Here is what I learned. Those friends who could not increase me would inevitably decrease me. In other words, my associations or buddies were like moving escalators. Every interaction with them caused me to progress in a given direction. I realized that I did not have any neutral friends. Each one caused me to either progress or regress, advance or decline, grow or stagnate. The Bible says:

> The heartfelt counsel of **a friend** is as sweet as perfume and incense (Proverbs 27:9).

Let me underscore at this point that real friends are not "yes" men or women who tiptoe around you, sugarcoating your behavior and singing your praises regardless of your conduct. That might feel nice for a while, but this type of friend will certainly not help you grow or mature. The Bible says:

> As iron sharpens iron, so **a friend** sharpens a friend (Proverbs 27:17).

The Hebrew word used for *friend* in that text is the word *aoyer*, which means "intimate associate." Real friends look you in the eye and "rub" against you to sharpen you. They are folks who will have the boldness to correct you when you get off track and who will spur you on when you feel weak. They are Cheerleaders! Cheerleaders is the subject of our next chapter.

Before you read on, why don't you pause for a moment and do what I did? Write down the names of your current friends and close associates.

Then ask yourself about each person, *Does this person add to me or take away from me? Do I grow from being around this person?* Be brutal with your findings. Don't panic if everyone on your list is disqualified. Just stay with me as we continue this life-changing journey together.

EVERY RELATIONSHIP IS LIKE A CURRENT THAT MOVES YOU TOWARD YOUR GOD-GIVEN ASSIGNMENT OR AWAY FROM IT.

ENDNOTE

1. Dennis D. Sempebwa, *You Have a Dream* (Peotone, IL: EWI, 2007).

CHAPTER PRINCIPLES

1. There is no such thing as a neutral friend.

2. You become like those who surround you.

3. Negative associations are contagious.

4. Godly relationships propel you toward your divine destiny.

5. When friendships don't add to your journey, they have become too expensive for you to maintain.

6. Every relationship is like a current that moves you toward your God-given assignment or away from it.

Chapter Two

CHEERLEADERS — ENTHUSIASTIC SUPPORTERS

To be without a friend is to be poor indeed.
— Tanzanian Proverb

The term *Cheerleaders* refers to an enthusiastic and vocal supporter— someone whose primary function is to encourage you; to tell you that "YOU CAN DO IT!"

The Bible says:

A friend loveth at all times, and a brother is born for adversity (Proverbs 17:17 KJV).

That's right! A friend does not disappear when things aren't going right. Ever see a cheerleading squad quit because their team is losing? Regardless of the score, they keep cheering, encouraging, "YOU CAN DO IT!"

The New Living Translation of the same verse puts it this way:

A friend is always loyal, and a brother is born to help in time of need.

My friends are my cheerleaders. I need them by my side during my good times, but especially during the bad times. When things are not going right, when my faith is weak, when I feel like throwing in the towel, they are there to shout me on—to cheer me to victory! They are folks who are close enough and bold enough to correct me when I get off track and spur me on when I feel weak.

Cheerleaders Are Called to Walk Alongside You.

Let's look at three characteristics of Cheerleaders:

1. Cheerleaders Celebrate Your Strengths

Proverbs 27:17 in the King James Version says:

> *Iron sharpeneth iron; so a man sharpeneth the countenance of his friend.*

Iron sharpening iron indicates a picture of equal contribution. One piece of iron is not necessarily better than the other. Cheerleaders are not coaches. They are not in your life to teach you, train you, instruct you, or guide you. They are there to sharpen and encourage you to better yourself. They notice when you are down, and don't stay quiet when you need encouragement. They remind you of God's hand on your life and cause faith to rise within you.

My number one Cheerleader is my wife, Ingrid. She encourages me when I feel frustrated and drained. She is sensitive to my needs and can often sense when I am not well. While everyone one else might be oblivious to my true disposition, she can always tell. She knows when to probe past the rhetorical, "I'm OK, Baby." One thing I so appreciate about her is that she has learned not to assume the role of a coach during those times I need her to simply cheer me on. She does not try to correct me, or fix me, or improve me. If she thinks I could benefit from some solid biblical exhortation, she will tactfully ask, "When did you last speak to Dr. Sumrall?" Or, "Have you spoken to Dr. Munroe about this?" She sends me to my Coaches.

Cheerleaders Are Encouragers.

Ingrid rises with me to enjoy the mountains in my life—the happy, victorious moments. She has also been with me in the darkest, most shameful moments of my life. I can always count on her. She is my Cheerleader.

2. Cheerleaders Cover Your Weaknesses

When a college football team is losing a game, the Cheerleading squad does not change its song or chant. They don't say, "You bunch of losers! You can't even hold up your end against this team. Shame on you!" On the contrary, the Cheerleaders keep encouraging the team, even to the last second.

The Bible says:

> *Though one may be overpowered, two can defend themselves.*
> *A cord of three strands is not quickly broken* (Ecclesiastes 4:12 NIV).

If one is found to be weak against an enemy, two shall succeed. In other words, the strength of the second covers the weaknesses or failures of the one. With each additional hand, the strength and effectiveness is multiplied. Here is how The Message Bible cites the words of wise King Solomon in Ecclesiastes 4:12:

> *By yourself you're unprotected. With a friend you can face the worst. Can you round up a third? A three-stranded rope isn't easily snapped.*

Do you have someone who claims to be a friend, yet constantly criticizes you and puts you down? Does he or she expose your weaknesses and highlight your mistakes to others? If yes, then you must re-examine the position you have given him or her in your life. This type of person is a Corruptor, not a true friend.

CHEERLEADERS PICK YOU UP WHEN YOU ARE DOWN.

Cheerleaders cover your weaknesses, faults, mistakes, and shortcomings. They stand with you, and together you can face the worst and emerge victorious!

Barry and Ted became friends at work after Barry's transfer into Ted's department. They have a lot in common, love of family, faith, and career. One day Barry was asked to present a new concept to the board members. Although it was his original idea, he was nervous about presenting it to this unusually tough audience. Ted took Barry out to lunch that day for a serious pep talk. Ted stressed Barry's assets and pumped up his confidence. Even though Ted was in the same department and he also came up with creative ideas, he put those facts aside to motivate and encourage his friend Barry. Thanks to Cheerleader Ted, Barry gave a exciting moving presentation that has since put him on the CEO's short list for a senior management position. And guess what. Ted did not think, *Gosh I wish that was me.* He is a true Cheerleader.

3. Cheerleaders Are Committed to You

Concerning one of the most powerful biblical examples of true friendship, the Bible says:

> *And Jonathan made a solemn pact with David, because he loved him as he loved himself* (1 Samuel 18:3).

Isn't that powerful? The King James Version of the same text tells us that Jonathan made a covenant with David because he loved him as his own soul. True Cheerleaders commit to love, protect, and remain in relationships through thick or thin. Later we see Jonathan's commitment tested when his father, Saul, pressures him to betray his friend. Saul tries to persuade Jonathan that David threatened his heritage and future (see 1 Sam. 20:31). Even so, Jonathan's loyalty remained unshaken. He was David's Cheerleader.

Ruth says to Naomi:

> *Don't ask me to leave you and turn back. I will go wherever you go and live wherever you live. Your people will be my people, and your God will be my God* (Ruth 1:16).

It is easy to be committed when there is agreement and everything is going well, but what about during hard times? In fact, there is no such thing as commitment without hardship. It is in the face of abandonment or betrayal that true commitment comes alive.

I remember when my wife and I needed to make a very hard ministry transition. Prior to the move, we had met and prayed with all of our friends; everyone seemed to be onboard with the change. They had spoken very encouraging words over our lives. We were so excited. All seemed to be going smoothly until shortly after we made the move. Then the people we had served so diligently began to attack our character. We were smeared and misrepresented around the world. Although we had gone through enough transitions and been around long enough to know that something like this might happen, what we did not expect was the abandonment and betrayal of some of our closest friends. *What happened? We thought you were onboard. You even spoke prophetically over us. You said you felt God was leading us and that you would be there for us no matter what. Was it all a lie?* we wondered.

Thus we learned a hard lesson. Even though our friends genuinely *cared* for us, they really were not *committed* to us. You see, being in agreement with us did not mean commitment. And unfortunately, commitment is often tested after we depart the shores of agreement.

COMMITMENT ONLY COMES ALIVE
IN TIMES OF TRIAL.

TRUE FRIENDS

I have lived through incredible times in my life here on earth. I was raised in a country where poverty, sickness, death, and heartache were commonplace for me. But I can truly say that through every season of my life, God sent me friends who loved me, protected me, and encouraged me to keep walking in spite of the overwhelming hardships. With my friends, I could go through anything. We could take on any adversary; and indeed we did! We protected each other, challenged each other, and even through excessive calamity, remained committed to the friendship God had given us. The Book of Proverbs says:

Friends come and friends go, but a true friend sticks by you like family (Proverbs 18:24 TM).

As long as I can recall, my true friends almost always moved in with me and my family—they became like brothers to me. God would knit my heart together with theirs—guys who had no family support structure or were under-privileged. My family was not well off by any means, but my mom always believed in sharing the little we had. So kids moved in and we became one large family. To this day, my long-time friend, Fred, is like a son to my mother. What a joy!

The Amplified Bible version of the same verse says:

The man of many friends [a friend of all the world] will prove himself a bad friend, but there is a friend who sticks closer than a brother (Proverbs 18:24).

This passage tells me that we can only have a handful of real friendships; that being intimately connected at a deep friendship level with many people results in bad friendship.

The Bible says:

Do a favor and win a friend forever; nothing can untie that bond (Proverbs 18:19 TM).

Jackie professes her commitment to Monica, her friend of 20 years. "I don't care what happens, I will never leave you. I know God has sent me into your life to love you and your family. We shall be friends for life." They weep as Monica embraces her.

Six months later, Monica's husband accepts a job transfer out-of-state. Jackie is hurt and takes the decision personally. "How could you do this to our friendship? You and Dan should have turned this down. What's more important, our friendship or a career opportunity?" Monica is speechless. In spite of her pleas, Jackie feels rejected and starts to pull back from their relationship. She refuses to answer Monica's calls, who is now completely devastated. Her decades'-long relationship with the person she called her best friend is over. What happened? When faced with separation, estrangement, and isolation, Jackie failed the test of commitment.

Friends will come and go for all sorts of reasons in life due to a variety of circumstances—career moves, change in family situations, difference of opinions or interests, just to name a few—but godly friendships aren't supposed to be that way. These are the friends who stand by you through diverse struggles and challenges. These are the relationships that become stronger over time. Pray that God will bring to you true friends who love you no matter what.

This chapter ends with a quote from an e-mail that a friend forwarded to me:

Oh the comfort—the inexpressible comfort of feeling safe with a person, having neither to weigh thoughts, nor measure words, but pouring them all out, just as they are, chaff and grain together; knowing that a faithful hand will take and sift them—keep what is worth keeping—and with the breath of kindness blow the rest away.

There are no more powerful words to describe a true Cheerleader.

In the next two chapters we will be examining nine critical questions that Christians should ask themselves about the people with whom they have chosen to walk through life.

Chapter Principles

1. Cheerleaders are called to walk alongside you.

2. Cheerleaders are encouragers.

3. Cheerleaders pick you up when you are down.

4. Commitment only comes alive in times of trial.

Chapter Three

NINE CRITICAL QUESTIONS (1–5)

Hold a true friend with both your hands.
                                            –Nigerian Proverb

Unlike my futile attempt to predetermine the good mangoes from the bad, there *are* ways that we can clearly decipher with whom to walk. I call these ways the Nine Critical Criteria for selecting Cheerleaders. Not everyone can be a Cheerleader because it takes more than friendship, it takes commitment. You must ask yourself nine questions about those with whom you chose to walk through life. Detailed in this chapter are questions one through five. Chapter 4 discusses the remaining four important questions.

#1: ARE THEY WALKING WITH GOD?

The psalmist declares:

> *...I'm a friend and companion of all who fear you, of those committed to living by your rules...* (Psalm 119:63 TM).

As a child of God, your Cheerleader's most important function is to encourage your walk with God. He or she must help you focus on what should be the most important relationship in your life—Jesus and you! Paul cautions:

> *Don't become partners with those who reject God. How can you make a partnership out of right and wrong? That's not partnership;*

that's war. Is light best friends with dark? (2 Corinthians 6:14 The Message)

I know that some of us have Cheerleaders who might not necessarily share the same maturity of faith as we do. They might be childhood friends or former schoolmates with whom we have shared life's detours. Even then, if they cause us to regress and stagnate in our faith walk, then they are simply too expensive for us to keep. In other words, continuing to walk intimately with them will prove too costly or even detrimental for our faith and well-being.

Your Cheerleaders must never replace God in your life. The moment they do, they become Corruptors. In fact, before we are anyone's friend, we must be God's first and foremost. James writes:

> *You adulterers! Don't you realize that friendship with this world makes you an enemy of God? I say it again, if you want to be a friend of the world, you make yourself an enemy of God* (James 4:4).

OUR FRIENDSHIP WITH GOD MUST TRANSCEND ALL EARTHLY FRIENDSHIPS.

Jesus must be the center of your life. He is first. He saved you. He redeemed you from eternal damnation. He must be first in your life. He ought to be your number one friend.

Regarding Job, God said to satan:

> *Have you noticed my friend Job? There's no one quite like him—honest and true to his word, totally devoted to God and hating evil* (Job 1:8 TM).

Ask yourself these questions: *When faced with daunting challenges, do my Cheerleaders push me to a place of faith in God and prayer? Do they encourage me to find my bearings in Him, and not in our friendship?* Writes former Dutch Prime Minister and preacher Abraham Kuyper, "He is your friend who pushes you closer to God."[1]

#2: Are They People of Character?

Writes Cicero, "We should measure affection, not like youngsters by the ardor of our passion, but by strength and constancy."[2] This is the second most important question to ask concerning your Cheerleaders. Is this a man or woman of character?

And what is character? It is described as a summation of the ideals by which you live your life. Character is all the mental and moral attributes, whether good or evil, that define you as an individual. Whether we are aware or not, character affects every area of your life—your decisions, words, actions, reactions, attitudes, goals, and your relationships. In fact, most failures—whether in marriage, habits, at the job, or in the church—can be traced back to a breakdown in character.

Proverbs 18:16 (NKJV) says that:

A man's gift makes room for him, and brings him before great men.

It is true that gifting or talent will most certainly cause doors to open before you, but only character keeps them open. Your character is the most vital factor in all decision making. I once heard someone say that when we wrap up our assignments here on earth, the only thing that cannot be buried with our corpses is our character. This is what we are when no one is watching.

Character is not built behind the pulpit or in the limelight. It is not acquired in a counseling room or signed off in a boardroom. One cannot receive character in a prayer line with the laying on of hands. It is not learned in a conference or seminar or taught in Bible school. Character is developed internally, when no one is watching.

Character Must Be the Defining Trait
in Our Friends' Lives.

The Bible says:

So we are lying if we say we have fellowship with God but go on living in spiritual darkness. We are not living in the truth (1 John 1:6).

Carefully examine your friends' character. Do not be fooled; it's what they do daily that defines them. It's their actions that create habits; habits form character and character determines where they will ultimately end up in life. Dr. Billy Graham said that, "When wealth is lost, nothing is lost; when health is lost, something is lost; when character is lost, all is lost."[3] How profoundly true!

Do you walk with men or women of integrity? Integrity, by the way, happens to be one of the most prominent byproducts of character. Let's discuss that.

The word *integrity* originates from a Latin word *integer*, which means "inner strength." In the Hebrew language, it's the word *tom*, which means "whole, sound, or unimpaired." Integrity can also be defined as moral soundness. It is the absence of duplicity. People of integrity are reliable, accountable, and internally solid. The Italians have a proverb that says, "Between saying and doing, many a pair of shoes is worn out." How true that is! The Bible says in the Book of Proverbs 12:22 (TM):

> God can't stomach liars; He loves the company of those who keep their word.

If your friends have integrity, they will live consistent lives. They are the same wherever they are whatever they're doing. True integrity does not end when they walk out of church, ministry offices, or into their private world. In many ways, that is where it really begins. That is when we must start to practice what we preach, to show who we truly are.

James wrote:

> Don't fool yourself into thinking that you are a listener when you are anything but, letting the Word go in one ear and out the other. Act on what you hear! Those who hear and don't act are like those who glance in the mirror, walk away, and two minutes later have no idea who they are, what they look like (James 1:22-24 TM).

If you embrace a friend who lacks character, you are headed for pain. David experienced this firsthand. He writes:

> It is not an enemy who taunts me—I could bear that. It is not my foes who so arrogantly insult me—I could have hidden from them. Instead, it is you—my equal, my companion and close

*friend. What good fellowship we once enjoyed as we walked to-
gether to the house of God* (Psalm 55:12-14).

#3: Are They Submitted to Authority?

Your Cheerleader must possess a heart of submission to authority.
There are five types of authority mentioned in the Bible. Let's briefly examine them individually and see how they affect our Cheerleaders.

1. Submission to God

James writes:

> *Submit yourselves therefore to God...* (James 4:7a KJV).

Submission to God is non-negotiable in the life of a true child of God.
My Cheerleaders must be first and foremost submitted to God and His
Word. They must love Jesus and His Church. They must want to reach
others for Him. They should love His house and be proud citizens of His
Kingdom—beacons of Christ's marvelous light in this perishing world.

The Bible says:

> *For this is as the Lord commanded us when he said, "I have made
> you a light to the Gentiles, to bring salvation to the farthest cor-
> ners of the earth"* (Acts 13:47).

As Christians, we are light to those who don't know Christ—the world.
Our primary assignment here on earth is to share the good news of Jesus
Christ and bring those around us to the revelation of His saving grace.

In the Book of Romans, Paul warns:

> *For they being ignorant of God's righteousness, and going about
> to establish their own righteousness, have not submitted them-
> selves unto the righteousness of God* (Romans 10:3 KJV).

Paul was referring to a group of people who thought that they could
work their way into God's favor by obeying the law. They had refused to
fully submit to the "righteousness of God." Consequently, they were out
of fellowship with Him and would ultimately suffer the same fate as unbelievers whose lives were characterized by unrighteousness.

In his second letter to the Corinthians, Paul writes:

Be ye not unequally yoked together with unbelievers: for what fellowship hath righteousness with unrighteousness? And what communion hath light with darkness? (2 Corinthians 6:14 KJV)

The word *communion* here is the Greek word, *metoche*, which means "fellowship or sharing." Another meaning is social intercourse or friendship.

Paul could not have been any clearer. He is saying here in the simplest of terms that those among us who know Christ and live truly submitted to Him—the believers—are very different from those who live in rebellion to His Word or non-believers. The Bible says that we are light, and they are darkness, and the two just cannot commune. Thus, it's vitally important to consider whether or not a Cheerleader lives a submitted life to God.

Godly Cheerleaders Have Christ as the Center of Their Lives.

---

2. Submission to Spiritual Authority

The writer of the Book of Hebrews says:

*Obey them that have the rule over you, **and submit yourselves: for they watch for your souls**...* (Hebrews 13:17 KJV).

Are your Cheerleaders submitted to their pastor, or the man or woman over their spiritual lives? Are they committed to a local body of believers, or are they church-hoppers? Peter advised:

*Likewise, ye younger, **submit yourselves unto the elder**...* (1 Peter 5:5 KJV).

To the young women, Paul writes:

Let the elders that rule well be counted worthy of double honour, especially they who labour in the word and doctrine (1 Timothy 5:17 KJV).

And we beseech you, brethren, to know them which labour among you, and admonish you... And to esteem them very highly in love for their work's sake. And be at peace among yourselves (1 Thessalonians 5:12-13 KJV).

These passages encourage young men and young women to be submitted to the elders within the Body of Christ. So if you walk closely to someone who gives no thought to spiritual authority, it's time to carefully reconsider the veracity of that relationship.

3. Submission to Delegated Authority

Paul told the Romans:

Everyone must submit to governing authorities. *For all authority comes from God, and those in positions of authority have been placed there by God. So anyone who rebels against authority is rebelling against what God has instituted, and they will be punished* (Romans 13:1-2).

The term *government* refers to a system by which a community or political unit is run or maintained. It also refers to our employers, instructors, teachers, the law, and anyone in authority over our earthly affairs. God put them over us, so their authority originates from Him. Dishonoring or refusing to submit to them is also tantamount to dishonoring Him who put them over us.

Do your Cheerleaders obey the law? Do they pay their taxes?

First Peter 2:13-15 (KJV) says:

Submit yourselves to every ordinance of man for the Lord's sake: *whether it be to the king, as supreme; or unto governors, as unto them that are sent by him for the punishment of evildoers, and for the praise of them that do well. For so is the will of God, that with well doing ye may put to silence the ignorance of foolish men.*

Peter could not have been clearer.

GODLY CHEERLEADERS ARE LAW-ABIDING
MEMBERS OF THEIR COMMUNITIES.

---

4. Submission to Parental Authority

The apostle Paul wrote:

> **Children, obey your parents** because you belong to the Lord,
> for this is the right thing to do. "Honor your father and mother."
> This is the first commandment with a promise: If you honor your
> father and mother, "things will go well for you, and you will
> have a long life on the earth" (Ephesians 6:1-3).

To godly Cheerleaders, submission to parental authority is not an option. It's a privilege and a blessing.

GODLY CHEERLEADERS ALWAYS MAINTAIN RESPECT
FOR THEIR EARTHLY PARENTS.

I must note, however, that parental submission is not always the same as parental obedience. In many societies or communities, obedience to God can mean disobedience to parents because believers often have to take positions that contradict cultural, traditional, and societal norms and beliefs. Remember, our ultimate counsel is God's Word, and our unquestionable allegiance belongs only to Him.

Notwithstanding, whether they agree with their parents or not, your Cheerleaders must always maintain a posture of respect for them and never dishonor them.

5. Submission to Spouses

Paul told the Ephesian church:

> Wives, submit yourselves unto your own husbands, as unto the
> Lord (Ephesians 5:22 KJV).

A few verses later in verse 25, he writes:

> Husbands, love your wives, even as Christ also loved the church,
> and **gave Himself for it**.

Contrary to the stereotypical view of the husband lording over the wife, submission in marriage is mutual. In fact, a godly marriage consists of two servants offering their gifts, abilities, affirmation, respect, and affection to each other for the good of their union. Although the man has the godly mandate to lead his home, he is not a slave master to his wife. In Ephesians 5:21, Paul talks about:

Submitting yourselves *one to another in the fear of God.*

The apostle Peter even puts it more bluntly. He writes:

In the same way, you husbands must give honor to your wives. Treat her with understanding as you live together. She may be weaker than you are, but she is your equal partner in God's gift of new life. If you don't treat her as you should, your prayers will not be heard (1 Peter 3:7).

If your Cheerleader is married, does he or she love and respect his or her spouse as an equal partner in God's gift of life? If not, it's time to encourage him or her to change—to do the Word of God, or you will not be able to maximize your relationship.

True Submission

I believe that true submission is a heart transformation issue. My parents grew up under the powerful Buganda Kingdom of Uganda. Obeying the king, his laws, and his appointed chiefs was never an option. Like other ancient monarchies, our king, King Mutesa II, had absolute power and unquestioned authority!

Then the British colonized Uganda and introduced a new system of government. They called it *democracy*—a government of the people, for the people, by the people. For the first time in our tribal history, the common man had a voice in this new form of government. Furthermore, they told us that if we did not like the laws or the new leaders, we could go to the polls and vote to change them. What a difference!

Most of Africa's problems today stem from her failure to adopt the correct manner of thinking. This could explain what might look like a reluctance to challenge oppressive dictators that have lorded over and destroyed the fabric of African democracies. As a people, we are not conditioned to debate, challenge, or question authority. Like subjects in a kingdom, our portion is to obey; to unquestioningly submit.

Christianity is not a democracy. It is a monarchy—it is God's Kingdom! When we become Christians, we become subjects in God's Kingdom. John 3:3 says:

> Jesus replied, "I tell you the truth, unless you are born again, you cannot see the Kingdom of God."

Paul announced:

> For at just the right time Christ will be revealed from heaven by the blessed and only almighty God, the King of kings and Lord of lords (1 Timothy 6:15).

Jesus Christ is not only a king but also the King of kings. The psalmist writes:

> How great is our Lord! **His power is absolute!** His understanding is beyond comprehension! (Psalm 147:5)

Just like monarchic societies cannot effectively practice democracy without fundamentally changing their thought patterns, it is impossible to understand kingdom principles with a democratic mindset. It is impossible to develop a heart of true submission without adopting Kingdom-thinking.

So examine your Cheerleaders' lives. Do they have submitted hearts? I really believe this to be one of the critical criteria for determining with whom to intimately walk.

#4: DO WE HAVE THE SAME VALUES?

Amos 3:3 (NKJV) asks a very important question:

> Can two walk together, except they be agreed?

Here the word *together* is the Hebrew term *yachad*, which means "properly, unitedly or as a unit." The question in Amos could be asked this way: "Can two people walk as a unit while heading in different directions?"

Your values are your non-negotiables—those things that you hold dear to your heart. That is why the first criterion of friendship with God is absolutely critical. As a believer, your values are dictated by God's

Word. If your friend does not care about Bible dictates, his or her value-base will be different from yours, and you will soon reach an impasse.

TRUE BELIEVERS HAVE CLEAR NON-NEGOTIABLES
DICTATED BY THE WORD OF GOD.

Most of us connect with people based on interests or hobbies. Your relationships will not strain over what you have in common, but the differences or what I call your distinctions! Relationships, even marriages, don't break up over similarities, but differences. For example, married couples don't drift apart over the things they enjoy doing together, but the peeves that privately irritate them and secretly erode at the core of their marital bond.

I believe that as Christians, God wants us to treat our Cheerleaders with respect and care. Paul writes:

> *When you hurt your friend, you hurt Christ* (1 Corinthians 8:12a TM).

So here is the question: What do you value? And then second, do you share the same values as the man and woman with whom you have decided to walk through life?

#5: DO WE HAVE THE SAME PRIORITIES?

Your values dictate your priorities. For example, as a family, we go to church on Sunday. That is part of our family credo—to gather with other believers for encouragement and to worship God together. Now imagine I have a best friend who has no relationship with God whatsoever. He thinks church is a complete waste of time; that Christianity is a joke. He believes that Sunday is relaxation day, or clean-up-around-the-house day. Do you think we can grow together?

I am not suggesting that our friends must like everything we like. But when the priorities are vastly different, then consideration needs to be made as to whether one can still walk alongside another. Says a proverb, "A man is known by the company he keeps."

ENDNOTES

1. http://en.wikiquote.org/wiki/Abraham_Kuyper

2. http://www.happypublishing.com/quotations/love-quotes.htm; accessed 3/4/10.

3. http://www.brainyquote.com/quotes/quotes/b/billy-graha161989.html; accessed 2/14/10.

CHAPTER PRINCIPLES

1. Our friendship with God must transcend all earthly friendships.

2. Character must be the defining trait in our friends' lives.

3. Godly cheerleaders have Christ as the center of their lives.

4. Godly cheerleaders are law-abiding members of their communities.

5. Godly cheerleaders always maintain respect for their earthly parents.

6. True believers have clear non-negotiables dictated by the Word of God.

Chapter Four

NINE CRITICAL QUESTIONS (6–9)

He that lies down with dogs shall rise with flies.
—Latin Proverb

By now you realize the importance of asking these questions about the ones you are considering bringing alongside you. The answers to these questions empower you to make the right choices that will keep you on the track toward success and fulfillment.

Let's look at the remaining questions, focusing especially on your dreams and destiny.

#6: DO THEY VALUE MY DREAM?

For 17 years I was part of a gospel music group from Uganda called Limit X. At a critical stage of our career in 1990, we felt that God was leading us to quit our secular jobs and go into full-time ministry. In the natural, that was a scary proposition, especially since at that time, we lived in one of the most expensive cities in the world—London, England.

As soon as we acted on our conviction, we had an onslaught of criticism from all quarters. Some of our closest friends called us lazy and irresponsible. They said that we had embarked on "a hopeless venture that was doomed to fail." They pressured us to find "real jobs" so we could make "something" of our lives.

Our response? We decided to stay away from them. We isolated ourselves and began to dream out loud. We talked about our amazing future success. We saw our music selling globally and imagined sharing stages with some of the people we admired. We saw all this great success before we had a single booking.

Consequently, within a relatively short period of time, we accomplished some incredible milestones. We released five albums and four radio singles, traveled to almost 40 nations, with our ministry calendar fully booked a year in advance; our songs became hits in multiple global markets. We ministered to live audiences of up to 500,000 people in a single event, performing before royalty, dignitaries, and heads of states in some of the most prestigious concert venues in the world like the Royal Albert Hall in London and Madison Square Gardens in New York. Limit X shared the stage with some of the world's most successful recording artists. We won music awards across the continents. Most importantly, we saw literally tens of thousands of lives begin their walk with Christ and experience His transforming power.

By God's grace, we accomplished more than we ever imagined. I am certain that had we not cut off those hindering, critical, and judgmental voices, you would not reading this book today.

The Bible says:

> Become wise by walking with the wise; hang out with fools and watch your life fall to pieces (Proverbs 13:20 TM).

I find this passage very interesting. The Bible is telling us that we become wise by walking with the wise. We don't have to be wise to begin with. We only need to walk with them. Conversely, we don't have to be fools to experience destruction. Merely walking with them leads us to calamity.

TRUE CHEERLEADERS WILL DREAM WITH YOU.

Do your friends value your dreams? What do they say when you share your plans for your financial future, for the dream house you and your wife wish to buy one day? What is their response when you try and articulate your vision for your ministry or your career? Do they listen to you, or even better, encourage you to dream bigger? Their response is a clear indication of their real place in your life, because true Cheerleaders will *dream with you.*

#7: DO THEY LAUGH WITH ME?

True friends will also *laugh with you*. They will ride the upward emotions of elation and joy with you. Simply put, they are happy when you are happy.

Rita and Paula met at a regional singles retreat for their church denomination. They seemed to hit it off immediately. They both happen to be small group leaders with their mega churches, and incidentally, also recovering from bitter divorces. For the first couple of months, they talked almost every night. They shared very similar marital histories, especially regarding their ex-husbands' habitual affairs, and mental and physical abuse. They sincerely believed that God brought them together to encourage one another and to journey together into His purpose for their lives—to be Cheerleaders for one another.

One day, Rita gets a very exciting phone call from her pastor—she is being promoted. Her singles group has exploded beyond her pastor's expectations. Consequently, he has recommended her for an opening on the district oversight board of their denomination. Rita will soon oversee 30 other singles groups within the district. She is beside herself, and cannot wait to tell her new friend about it.

When she breaks the news to Paula, however, there is silence. Paula is livid. "Why didn't that happen to me? I have been doing this a lot longer than you...and frankly speaking, I don't feel you deserve it. This might sound harsh but I gotta tell ya, you just haven't paid your dues yet, Rita."

Rita is devastated. She thought that in Paula she had a Cheerleader, someone who rooted for her and would be really happy for her promotion.

*So Jesus told them this story: "If a man has a hundred sheep and one of them gets lost, what will he do? Won't he leave the ninety-nine others in the wilderness and go to search for the one that is lost until he finds it? And when he has found it, he will joyfully carry it home on his shoulders. When he arrives, **he will call together his friends** and neighbors, saying, 'Rejoice with me because I have found my lost sheep.' In the same way, there is more joy in heaven over one lost sinner who repents and returns to God than over ninety-nine others who are righteous and haven't strayed away! "Or suppose a woman has ten silver coins and loses one. Won't she light a lamp and sweep the entire house and search*

*carefully until she finds it? And when she finds it, **she will call
in her friends** and neighbors and say, 'Rejoice with me because
I have found my lost coin.' In the same way, there is joy in the
presence of God's angels when even one sinner repents"* (Luke
15:3-10).

Watch your friends' facial expressions when you share a recent victory. Listen to their tone of voice when you share your testimony. Are they genuinely excited for you? Do they laugh with you?

TRUE CHEERLEADERS WILL LAUGH WITH YOU.

#8: DO THEY CRY WITH ME?

Tiffany gets home after a long day at work. She is exhausted from all the sales meetings and just wants to turn in early. She cannot help but notice the pile of dirty dishes in her sink and the extra-full laundry hamper. "Everything can wait till tomorrow," she retorts. As she leans over her nightstand to set the alarm clock, she hears the digital answering machine going off downstairs. This is the sixth time it's gone off in the last hour. Someone is really trying to contact her. Very reluctantly, she decides to go check the messages.

She has 13 missed calls, all from the same number. *It's Melody! What could be wrong?* she wonders, as she fumbles to call her friend back.

Melody is frantic! Phil, her husband of 15 years, is having an affair. She caught him in many lies recently, and finally confronted him last night. He admits it. Although he sounds sorry and has promised to seek help, she is devastated. They have three great kids and a growing ministry. She doesn't even have the words to express her pain.

Tiffany gives no thought to her fatigue and exhaustion. She slips on her jeans, grabs an overnighter, and rushes out to comfort her friend. She is a Cheerleader. She cries with her best friend.

TRUE CHEERLEADERS WILL CRY WITH YOU.

Paul writes:

> *Share each other's troubles and problems, and in this way obey the law of Christ* (Galatians 6:2).

Notice that Paul did not say to *remove* one another's burdens. There are times when our friends go through seasons of untold stress or emotional weight. The Bible instructs us to literally get underneath the loads, troubles, and problems of others and *share* the weight.

True friends will dream with you, laugh with you, but also cry with you. In other words, they live life with you. An African proverb states, "A friend is someone you share the path with."

#9: WHERE ARE THEY GOING?

The final question we have to ask of those we walk with is, "Where are you going?"

There are three types of people:

1. Carefree Charlie

Charlie is a simple guy, who doesn't like to bother thinking about how he is actually going to walk out his life. He is happy to go wherever the winds of life blow, following crowds, embracing new fads and trends, wherever they might take him. Charlie generally tries to fit in with all the other Joes-on-the-block.

True Cheerleaders don't merely "go with the flow," as the cliché goes. In fact, most of them go against it. They look ahead. They prepare. They plan. Walk with such a person, and your life will prosper. Happy-go-lucky people who live aimlessly, purposelessly with no sense of tomorrow whatsoever will drag you down. In his book *The Principles and Power of Vision*, Dr. Myles Munroe writes: "The real problem is the color of people's lives; their lives are 'gray.' Such people don't have a precise way of living. They're just here. They drift along, allowing life to happen to them." The Bible says:

> *Look straight ahead, and fix your eyes on what lies before you.*
> **Mark out a straight path for your feet; stay on the safe path.**
> *Don't get sidetracked* (Proverbs 4:25-27a).

2. Busy Benny

Rather than just sitting by and doing nothing, Busy Benny grabs at everything around him. He changes jobs like dress shirts. He church-hops and has very shallow, short-lived relationships. This is because he doesn't stay anywhere long enough to build the necessary foundations to enjoy the fruits of relationship. Unlike Carefree Charlie, Busy Benny is active, but hardly effective; he pursues much but accomplishes little or nothing.

In his book *See You at the Top*,[1] Zig Ziglar tells a story about a French naturalist John Henry Fabre who conducted a fascinating experiment concerning this subject. Fabre arranged Processional Caterpillars in a circle around the rim of a flowerpot so that the lead caterpillar actually touched the last one, making a complete circle. In the center of the flowerpot he put pine needles, which is their food. The caterpillars started around this circular flowerpot. Around and around they went, hour after hour, day after day, and night after night. For seven full days and seven full nights they went around the pot. Finally, they dropped dead from starvation and exhaustion.

These poor caterpillars starved to death with an abundance of food less than six inches away, simply because they confused activity with accomplishment.

The Bible says:

> *Trust in the Lord with all your heart and lean not on your own understanding;* **in all your ways** *acknowledge Him,* **and He will make your paths** *straight* (Proverbs 3:5-6 NIV).

I live in perhaps the most over-gratified and impatient society in world history. It is a society of microwaves, remote control gadgets, high speed Internet, fast food restaurants, instant messaging, and meals to go. "Dear God, I pray for patience, but please, I want it right now," seems to be the prayer of the modern-day American Christian.

You are going to meet a fair amount of Busy Bennys. Don't be afraid to ask the important question: "Friend, where are you going?" If he or she is aimless, guess what? You are both headed for trouble. Retailer J.C. Penney said, "Give me a stock clerk with a goal and I will give you a man who will make history. Give me a man with no goals and I will give you a stock clerk."[2]

3. Purposeful Peter

Purposeful Peter thinks long-term. He lives with a driving sense of purpose. He is going somewhere, and the Bible calls him wise:

> *The prudent understand where they are going, but fools deceive themselves* (Proverbs 14:8).

Henry's friend, Lee, calls him with a prayer request. "Henry, this is it! It's the dream job of my life and I am a hair away from getting it. Please, please believe God with me. I really need to make a good impression with my interviewer tomorrow. I believe this job opens up everything I have dreamed of and gets me on the right track to doing what God has assigned for me." Being a true friend, Henry decides to seriously take Lee's request to God in prayer. In fact, he decides to fast a whole day and pray for his friend.

Days roll into weeks, and no word from Lee. Henry finally calls to ask, eager to know what happened. "Lee, how'd it go? Get the job?" asks Henry.

"Job...what job?" Lee responds.

"You know, the dream job you shared with me about three weeks back."

Lee pauses completely oblivious. Finally, he says, "O that job...yeah, well, I woke up the following day and thought, *Nah, I'm not into that. God has something better for me.* So I am waiting for a call back about this other opportunity. Please, please keep this one lifted up in prayer. This one is really it, Henry."

Henry is perplexed. This is not the first time Lee has done this. If it's not his jobs, it's the girlfriends that he believes have been sent by God to him. And what about all the missionary opportunities he feels called to, but has never really gone on any? Dale Carnegie observed: "The man who starts going nowhere generally gets there."[3] I like to say it like this: If you aim to shoot at nothing you won't miss.

The question you must ask is this: does this person I call friend, associate, companion, make me stronger or weaker? Does this guy or gal cause me to grow and advance toward my God-given purpose?

CHEERLEADERS ARE LIKE ESCALATORS.
THEY ADVANCE YOU TOWARD YOUR ASSIGNED DESTINY.

But let me briefly add this caution: finding real Cheerleaders (true friends) takes time. It does not mean you dismantle your relationships right away. Remember that you did not build them overnight. Thus it is not realistic to think that you will build positive ones instantly. The process takes time and focus.

If you have not done so already, I encourage you to make an honest assessment of the people around you. Again, don't be surprised to find that most of them are what I call, the *Then People*. They have known you for years. They like reminiscing about the good old days; how things used to be. Some even have a very hard time appreciating your current life station. Their primary wish is to have the "old you" back.

Regardless how many years you've known them, it's time for change. It's time to maximize your horizontal relationships and find your Cheerleaders; when you do, hold on to them. Love them and walk faithfully with them. The Bible says:

> *Do a favor and win a friend forever; nothing can untie that bond* (Proverbs 18:19 TM).

ENDNOTES

1. Zig Ziglar, *See You at the Top* (Gretna, LA: Pelican Publishing, 2000).

2. http://www.evancarmichael.com/Famous-Entrepreneurs/1026/JC-Penney-Quotes.html; accessed 2/15/10.

3 http://www.brainyquote.com/quotes/authors/d/dale_carnegie.html; accessed 2/15/10.

CHAPTER PRINCIPLES

1. True cheerleaders will dream with you.

2. True cheerleaders will laugh with you.

3. True cheerleaders will cry with you.

4. Cheerleaders are like escalators. They advance you toward your assigned destiny.

SECTION II

Vertical Relationships

In choosing a friend, go up a step.
–Jewish Proverb

Chapter Five

Two Schools of Learning

Advise and counsel him; if he does not listen,
let adversity teach him.

–Ethiopian Proverb

I honestly believe that life is designed in such a way that you don't have time to live your life out, make all the hurtful mistakes, learn from them, and still have enough time left to reach your destiny and live to your full potential. This is why we must pay attention to the next type of relationship—Vertical Relationships.

Vertical relationships involve the transfer of knowledge, wisdom, and experience from one individual to another. As you walk through life, God will send people who are interested in helping you get to the next step of your life. He also sends others to learn from you. They look at your mistakes and successes, and take notes. This is the subject of discussion in Section II.

I believe that God ordains life-teachers to train and equip us with the tools necessary to enter the next season of our development. There are two Schools of Learning: the School of Experience and the School of Instruction.

THERE ARE TWO SCHOOLS OF LEARNING:
EXPERIENCE AND INSTRUCTION.

THE SCHOOL OF EXPERIENCE

Allow me to introduce you to the School of Experience or SOE. The driving philosophy behind this school: *God sends hardships and challenges to teach us His ways.*

SOE students believe that *experience* is the primary way God teaches us about life and it is how He reveals His will to us. These students enjoy three primary enrollment advantages.

A Popular School

Think about it. SOE students have billions of classmates all around the world. The School of Hard Knocks, as my friends in Los Angeles call it, is simply the most common way people learn about life. As life happens to all of us, we hopefully extract lessons that help us avoid mistakes and maybe eventually lead us to success.

Easy Enrollment

One does not need to qualify for enrollment into the School of Experience. Just live. Take risks, make mistakes, get hurt, and simply keep living. The lessons present themselves as you walk through life.

Free Tuition

You don't have to pay anything to get into the School of Experience. It costs you nothing upfront. In other words, tuition is absolutely 100 percent free! Once again, just live and learn!

I used to be an enthusiast of this school until I started to look around. You see, throughout my childhood I often heard people say, "Experience is the best teacher...Experience is the best teacher." Well, now that I have been around a bit longer, I have discovered how untrue that is.

Barbara is in love. She's been going steady with her boyfriend for more than a year and so far has avoided any real intimate physical contact. He says he loves her and that after they graduate from high school, they will get married and live happily ever after. Barbara's mother, Sara, is a single mother raising two children. Sara tries to talk to Barbara about life and not becoming too serious about her boyfriend—she desperately wants Barbara to learn from her instruction rather than having Barbara experience the heartache that accompanies divorce and hard work that single-parenting is.

But instead, Barbara enrolls in SOE, gives in to her boyfriend's demands, gets pregnant, and is on the way to learning some of life's harshest lessons.

EXPERIENCE HAS NEVER BEEN GOD'S CHOSEN
METHOD OF INSTRUCTION.

Experience has never been God's chosen method of instruction. Here is why:

Non-retention

SOE students expect to make the mistakes first, and then maybe learn from them. I say, "maybe," because we all know that negative experiences don't necessarily teach us anything. In fact, most of us don't learn from our mistakes. We keep banging our heads against the same walls or issues, time and time again.

Cost

Although enrollment is free, the cost can be astronomical. SOE students usually end up losing their marriages, being torn apart from their loved ones, becoming unemployed, sick, broke, and so on. And again, the sad thing is that most of us experience all of these heartaches without learning a single lesson.

Scars

Quite often, the wounds received from experiencing life's lessons produce permanent scars. You might not always be able to remarry that spouse you drove away by your infidelity, reunite with your estranged daughter, or recoup the financial nest egg you lost due to your lack of integrity and poor character. You might have to bear the scars throughout the rest of your life. Unfortunately, some scars leave deep and devastating reminders, even after the lessons have been embraced.

As someone once said, experience is a hard teacher. You see, experience gives the test *before* the lesson. In other words, experience will harshly examine you regarding a lesson that you have not yet learned. For example, whereas facing bankruptcy could teach you how to better handle your finances, wouldn't you wish you had the opportunity to learn how to manage your money *before* being harshly tested in that manner?

EXPERIENCE IS A HARSH INSTRUCTOR
WHO CRITIQUES BEFORE SHE TEACHES.

God does not send hardships and challenges to teach us His ways. He gave us His written Word, the Bible, and He sent us the Holy Spirit who is ever present to help us through life. There is a solution in God's Word for any problem we will ever face. He loves us so very much that He provides a way to avoid troubles *before* we have to go through them. And He is faithful enough that if we find ourselves in trouble, He will show us the way out. Paul says:

> *The temptations in your life are no different from what others experience. And God is faithful. He will not allow the temptation to be more than you can stand. When you are tempted, He will show you a way out so that you can endure* (1 Corinthians 10:13).

Do you really think that experience is God's first choice for teaching His beloved children? Show me a father who puts his kids' fingers on a smoldering red-hot iron to teach them not to touch it, and I will show you a heartless child abuser. If we humans know better, what do we expect of our loving heavenly Father? The Bible says:

> *The prudent understand where they are going.... A prudent person foresees danger and takes precautions. The simpleton goes blindly on and suffers the consequences* (Proverbs 14:8; 22:3).

THE SCHOOL OF INSTRUCTION

Now let's look at the next School of Learning—the School of Instruction or SOI. The driving philosophy of this school: God ordains instructors to train and equip us with the necessary tools to enter the next season of our development.

The Bible says:

> *The tongue of the wise makes knowledge appealing, but the mouth of a fool belches out foolishness* (Proverbs 15:2).

INSTRUCTION IS GOD'S FIRST CHOICE OF LEARNING.

God desires that we posture as students or learners from those who have gone ahead of us. Notwithstanding, enrollment at SOI has its challenges.

SOI Is Not Popular

Walking down the road of instruction is lonely. You must determine to deafen your ears to the status quo. It's not easy to get into SOI because information about it is not readily available. Inquiries will most likely lead you to the more popular School of Learning—SOE. From SOE students you will hear remarks like:

"Oh, why bother about it? Just go with the flow."

"Roll with the dice mate… Que sera sera…"

"Don't worry about it. You will cross that bridge when you get there."

"Just chill out, buddy! Things will somehow fall into place."

There Is No Graduation

Enrollment in this school is indefinite. SOI students never get to graduate because successful people are on a constant quest for learning. There never comes a day when a diligent student of this school says, "Oh, I'm done now. I'm finished with instruction. Now I know everything I need to know." Henry Ford said, "Anyone who stops learning is old, whether at twenty or eighty. Anyone who keeps learning stays young."[1]

No Free Tuition

The School of Instruction is not free. In Proverbs 12:1 (TM), we read:

> *If you love learning, you love **the discipline that goes with it**— how shortsighted to refuse correction!*

The New Living Translation says:

*To learn, **you must love discipline**....*

Learning in this school will cost you discipline.

Most cultures believe that old age is rich with wisdom. Our fathers and mothers know what works and what doesn't. They have tasted the bitter fruit of impulsiveness, impatience, laziness, lack of self-control, and all manner of foolishness, and often have deep scars to show for their hard journey. They have thick mental notebooks about life. Many are wise, but the one thing they don't have is time. Though they know what to do, the opportunity to do it is long gone. Unfortunately, life is not a dress rehearsal. You only have one shot at it. After the clock turns, those seconds or minutes are buried in history, never to return.

Brad is in love. He's been going steady with his girlfriend for more than a year and so far has avoided any real intimate physical contact. She says she loves him and that after they graduate from high school, they will get married and live happily ever after. Brad's mother, Sue, is a single mother raising two children. Sue talks to Brad about life and not becoming too serious about his girlfriend—she desperately wants Brad to learn from her instruction rather than having Brad experience the heartache that accompanies divorce and hard work that single-parenting is.

Brad listened to his mother, enrolled in SOI, and learned about life in a disciplined and intelligent manner. He and his girlfriend finished high school and college, married, and are enjoying raising their family together.

So here is what we need to do—find that experienced coach, that seasoned mentor, that good autobiography, those prized memoirs, and study them. Observe the ways these people handled life—notice what they did right, paying particular attention to their mistakes and how they dealt with them. The Bible says:

*Just ask the previous generation. **Pay attention to the experience of our ancestors*** (Job 8:8).

You and I will save a tremendous amount of unnecessary pain and irredeemable time when we choose to enroll at God's School of Instruction.

Instruction Is a Kind Instructor
Who Equips You Before the Test.

King Solomon, the smartest man to walk this earth, advises:

Take good counsel and accept correction—that's the way to live wisely and well (Proverbs 19:20 TM).

In conclusion, let me quote one of my mentors, Dr. Wayne Cordeiro, pastor of New Hope Christian Fellowship in Hawaii. He has taught me a lot about this subject and has written extensively concerning this important success key. He empowers his congregation to become active learners and participants in all aspects of the ministry. Wayne's observations have helped make New Hope one of America's largest churches:

Success doesn't happen by accident; people don't stumble onto it by mistake. There are solid reasons why certain men and women are successful, and they leave clues behind for us to observe and collect—if we will look for them. A willing student of life will examine these clues and learn.... You will choose between two teachers in life: Wisdom and Consequence.[2]

CHOOSING WISDOM

When you choose to enroll in the School of Instruction, you choose to forego the hard knocks that come through the School of Experience. Learning from others what works and what doesn't work is the better road to travel. Life's journey need not be bumpy and full of potholes that damage your frame, halt your forward motion, and cause you distress. Life's journey can be smooth sailing under pleasant skies when you know how to avoid the bumps and skim over the holes—because you have learned from kind instructors who want you to succeed.

You must be willing to accept instruction—to become a Conduit. This role is critical when learning how to surround yourself with the right people. The next chapter provides a comprehensive discussion about Conduits.

ENDNOTES

1. John Maxwell, *The Power of Attitude* (Tulsa, OK: River Oak Publishing, 2001), 42.

2. Wayne Cordeiro, *The Dream Releasers* (Ventura, CA: Regal Books, 2002).

CHAPTER PRINCIPLES

1. There are two Schools of Learning: Experience and Instruction.

2. Experience has never been God's chosen method of instruction.

3. Experience is a harsh instructor who *critiques before* she teaches.

4. Instruction is God's first choice of learning.

5. Instruction is a kind instructor who *equips you before* the test.

Chapter Six

Become a Conduit

If you refuse the advice of an elder you will walk until sunset.
                                                    –Kenyan Proverb

Like a vertical scale that has upward and downward measurements, there are two kinds of Vertical Relationships—Conduits and Coaches. In this chapter, we will discuss Conduit relationships.

A *conduit* is a channel that carries a substance from one place to another. The term also refers to a means of conveying information from one source to another. Other names for Conduits include apprentices, protégés, disciples, sons, daughters, and students. These are folks who sit by a mentor or coach to learn or glean from him or her. Paul says:

> *Wherefore I beseech you, be ye followers of me* (1 Corinthians 4:16 KJV).

The Greek word used for the term followers in this text is the word, *mimhth*, which means "an imitator." Paul advises the Corinthians to imitate him, in other words, to become attentive students of his life and ways. The New Living Translation of this verse reads:

> *So I urge you to imitate me.*

Conduits Are Life Students Dedicated to Sitting
at the Feet of Seasoned Coaches.

We all need people who will challenge, affirm, correct, or validate us. Now and again, God will place our faces or names on mentors' hearts for a special purpose and particular season, so they can help us carry our visions to maturity.

Back in Uganda, during school holidays, my parents would sometimes send us to my grandparent's house in the village. There we played, mingled, and bonded with our cousins all day. But we also learned about our culture—the Baganda culture. We were taught who our ancestors were and heard stories of incredible bravery and courage. We learned about old tribal wars and intercultural conflicts with neighboring clans. We were taught the idioms and proverbs that form the basis of the value systems of our tribe. What a pivotal time! To this day, I live by many of those lessons. They form the bedrock for my personal code of ethics.

Why Become a Conduit?

What motivates people to seek out counsel, help, and direction from those ahead of them? Why should a young person decide to reach out to an elder instead of "toughing it out," as they like to say. There are three main reasons.

1. To Destroy Goliath

Goliath represents the habit, issue, or challenge that keeps knocking you down. This is the main reason why most people reach out to someone who has gone ahead of them for help. They are seeking guidance or help with challenging issues that, like Goliath, continually delay their developmental journey.

Everyone Has a Goliath.

2. To Reach a Higher Plateau

There is a saying, "Advice sharpens a rusty opinion." Have you stopped growing? Then you must consider that it is probably time to sit down at the feet of an experienced traveler. Oftentimes, plateaus are caused by behavioral blind spots. These are issues completely inconspicuous to us. They hold us back from journeying to our divine destiny. Until we find someone else who has been where we desire to be, we may never learn how to push through certain growth barriers.

BLIND SPOTS ARE INCONSPICUOUS
TO THE ONE WHO HAS THEM.

---

3. To Overcome a Lack of Confidence

Although most of us know what to do in order to grow into our assignments, we don't do it because we fear we might fail. Whether it's the fear of approaching your boss for that promotion that is long overdue, or apprehension in applying for those surplus funds in the company budget for your project, or standing up to the bossy, chauvinistic bureaucrats in the marketing department, most of us stand back from our destinies because of a lack of confidence. Most of these tough calls take a tremendous amount of courage and tact. Posturing as a Conduit protects you from going blindly into a hungry lion's month.

Becoming a Conduit assures your forward movement. No longer do you need to stay in the same place in life, your career, your relationships—learning from others who have excelled in these areas brings confidence and slays Goliath.

ROADBLOCKS

Most people know how vital it is to have a mentor, so why don't more people ask for advice? What stops us from finding coaches and sitting at their feet? Why do some of us feel we should reinvent the wheel and endure the same hurt as those who have gone before us? Well, here are some roadblocks for you to consider and learn to overcome.

1. Ignorance

The number one enemy of Conduits is ignorance. People just don't know the value in learning from Coaches. The old adage "What you don't know can't hurt you" is so erroneous! It is an undisputed fact that what you don't know can and will hurt you. The Bible says:

My people are destroyed for lack of knowledge... (Hosea 4:6 NKJV).

The phrase "My people" refers to those who know Him; His children, not the unbelievers. Isn't it interesting that He did not say, "My people are destroyed by lucifer and his demons"? It's because satan has already been defeated. The Bible says:

That is why the Scriptures say, "When He ascended to the heights, He led a crowd of captives and gave gifts to His people" (Ephesians 4:8).

John writes:

Ye are of God, little children, and have overcome them: because greater is He that is in you, than he that is in the world (1 John 4:4 KJV).

So our primary concern should not be the devil or demons, poverty, persecution, but *ignorance*. Ignorance not only hurts us, but it can destroy us. The Bible says in Proverbs 24:5 (NKJV):

...Yes, a man of knowledge increases strength.

Although being strong doesn't guarantee victory, it prepares you for it, just as going to medical school doesn't guarantee a successful medical career, but readies you for it. I often tell my students that enrolling in a Bible college doesn't guarantee that they will have successful ministries or churches. It only prepares them for it. The faculties and halls of great Bible training institutions or seminaries have many very knowledgeable men and women of God. Unfortunately you will find that some of these professors are unhappy, unfulfilled, and impoverished. Why? Because they teach knowledge but not its application. In fact, gaining knowledge only equips you for success.

KNOWLEDGE WITHOUT APPLICATION
LEADS TO FRUSTRATION.

Naturally we are afraid of what we don't know or cannot explain. It takes faith to invite someone else into our lives to help us walk out our purpose. So a good place to begin is on your knees in prayer. Ask God to give you faith and courage.

Did you know that the word *disciple* comes from the Greek word *math-ay-tes'*, which means "learner, pupil or student?" Thus the dedication to a process of study and learning is a basic function of a true disciple of Jesus Christ. We must be open to fresh knowledge in order to keep growing.

2. Pride

It is written:

It's common knowledge that "God goes against the willful proud; God gives grace to the willing humble" (James 4:6b TM).

Pride is perhaps the main reason why most people, particularly ministers, do not commit to gleaning from others. They are simply too proud to bow their knee. I have had ministers openly say to me, "No man can tell me what to do. I don't listen to anyone. I only listen to God." What pride and folly!

GOD WILL OFTEN ASSIGN PEOPLE TO LEND US A HAND
AND THUS SAVE US YEARS OF MISTAKES AND FOOLISHNESS.

I remember struggling with a very anointed young man a few years back. When seasoned ministers came around him, they could easily see God's hand on his life and were quick to tell him. Unfortunately, that caused him to become proud. He stopped listening to any counsel and proceeded to prematurely launch out into full-time ministry. It was a disaster. This is why Paul advises:

Likewise, ye younger, submit yourselves unto the elder...
(1 Peter 5:5 KJV).

Every time I have launched into major change, I reach out to my Coaches and posture as a Conduit. I plead, "Please be brutal with me. Don't just tell me what I want to hear. What am I missing? What should I prepare for? Does this sound like God to you? Am I on the right track?" Consequently, I have enjoyed a steady ride to God's best for my life. I can also trace my failures and disappointments to the lack of counsel and advice.

3. Fear

I remember the first time I had to go up to someone and ask to be mentored. I was nervous, eager, anxious, awkward, but also excited. What a range of emotions! What if he says no? What if he doesn't have the time? What if he asks me to do something that I can't do? Then what? What if I am not coaching material? All these questions were going through my mind. I was a nervous wreck. I was in fear. Here is an interesting Scripture that will calm your mind and destroy your fears.

Trust in the Lord with all your heart; do not depend on your own understanding (Proverbs 3:5).

WALKING INTO YOUR DESTINY WILL OFTEN CALL
FOR YOU TO LEARN FROM GOD THROUGH OTHERS.

No matter who you are or where you are in life, you will reach a point on your journey when you could use a "helping hand" or godly instruction to help you navigate through different situations and seasons.

Over the past 25 years, I have been through many seasonal changes. Without posturing as a Conduit, I would not be anywhere near where God has me today. I can say without a doubt that this is the best growth secret I have discovered aside from learning to listen to the Counselor Himself, the Holy Spirit. Paul encourages the Philippians:

Dear brothers and sisters, pattern your lives after mine, and learn from those who follow our example (Philippians 3:17).

The Japanese have a saying, "Feed a dog for three days and it is grateful for three years. Feed a cat for three years and it forgets after three days." All sensible people know the importance of sitting at the feet of a Coach. But simply wanting it does not mean one is ready for it. I have had numerous people ask, "Dr. Dennis, will you please coach me. I want to be you protégé. I want to be your disciple. I know that if you speak into my life, I will succeed." Years ago, I would quickly say, "Be glad to, mate. When do we begin?" After many a frustrating coaching relationship, I don't jump in too quickly these days. I have discovered that not everyone who says he or she is ready to be coached or disciplined really is. Shakespeare wrote, "Give every man thine ear, but few thy voice."

CONDUITS, NOT PARASITES

Let me tell you about Parasites. A Parasite is a plant or animal that lives on or in another, usually larger, host organism in a way that harms or is of no advantage to the host. Although both Conduit and Parasites attach to the Coach to glean and advance, the two are vastly different. Conduits attach to grow, to mature, and to eventually exact a bountiful return in the life of the Coach, whereas Parasites are only interested in themselves and their personal well-being. They attach to take and to use.

Be careful not to fall into the trap of being a Parasite. Consider your motives and attitude frequently so you know for sure that you are, intentionally or unintentionally, not draining your Coach. Be acutely aware of your relationship, and continually assess that it is mutually beneficial— that you are maturing because of the interaction with your mentor.

CONDUITS ATTACH TO GROW, PARASITES ATTACH TO DRAIN.

SIX CONDUIT ATTRIBUTES

Let's examine six critical attributes that define Conduits and identify Parasites.

#1: An Open Book

Jack, an elderly pastor, thinks he found his successor in Tim, his youth minister, only to realize after eight years of mentoring that the promising apprentice has his own agenda. Jack's secretary accidentally stumbled upon Tim's personal e-calendar. Evidently, Tim is trying to leave their small-town church for a position in a mega-church in the big city. He has privately been interviewed by the senior leadership there for the past several months. Jack sobs at the realization that the young protégé he cared for and poured so much into was only there to take. He was coaching a Parasite!

Real Conduits are transparent. They are open books and strive to live their lives out in front of those assigned to guide them. Parasites are pretentious or manipulative. They often hide relevant or pertinent issues from the one committed to helping them reach their potential.

TRUE CONDUITS ARE OPEN BOOKS.

Real Conduits are transparent about their shortcomings, aspirations, and dreams. A Coach can really help this type of person become all that God intended.

#2: A Likeable Demeanor

I like receiving e-mails from some of the young leaders I coach. Every morning, I wake up to about 40 personal e-mails from friends, our global network of leaders, and churches overseas. Although I am eager to read them all, I am at the edge of my seat when reading from a young protégé in Africa or India. In fact, I often open those first. I look forward to communicating with them. I want to hear how they are doing. It's a joy to walk with them because they are so open to all that God wants to reveal to them. They are friendly and their e-mails are fun to read.

Conduits have likeable demeanors and are pleasant to teach and instruct. The fact is, for someone to willingly and continually invest in anyone, it is helpful that they are likeable. Conduits strive to be as pleasant as possible. Remember this Conduits: your coach knows your flaws. It is pointless trying to make yourself look better than you really are.

A GODLY CONDUIT IS A PLEASURE TO INSTRUCT.

I need to mention that there is a difference between having a likeable demeanor and what they call "brown-nosing"—being nice just for the moment or impressing someone with faux friendliness. Remember that Conduits are likeable, while Parasites are pretentious and duplicitous. A mature Coach will "smell" the difference from miles away.

#3: A Pliable Disposition

A good friend recently told me about an apprentice he was attempting to mentor in a certain area. At first, the young man seemed keen to learn. He was fast and sharp, which is exciting. But after only one training session, the apprentice began to correct him. He offered off-the-wall advice and actually started to instruct my friend. In his immaturity, he believed he was ready to instruct the instructor.

One of the most frustrating things for any teacher is a cocky, know-it-all pupil. In his ignorance and immaturity, the student questions and debates the seasoned instruction of his teacher, forgetting his limitations. Parasites want to learn what they can as fast as they can—to use the instructor for purely selfish reasons.

True Conduits are not rigid and stuck in their ways. They are not opinionated and wiseacres. They don't let their prejudices stop them from receiving the guidance to grow and maximize their potential. They know who they are in the relationship. Conduits want to learn, to glean, and to mature. The Coach is the teacher, and the Conduit is the student. It is impossible to coach someone who thinks he or she knows better than you do. Can anyone really lead another who thinks his way is the better way? The Chinese have a saying, "When the student is ready, the teacher will appear." I have found that to be true. When the Conduit is ready to learn, to mold, to be formed, God sends a Coach into his or her life.

#4: A Respectful Posture

Pastor James runs a great inner city church. It seems as though God is adding scores of people to the congregation every week. His evangelism director, Jimmy, is an on-fire young leader who just graduated from Bible school. Every week, Jimmy hits the streets and fearlessly introduces the lost, the broken, and the thirsty to God's saving grace. It's harvest time!

Pastor James begins to feel that perhaps he really needs to pour his heart into Jimmy. "Hey, young Jimmy might even take my place one day, since I am continually being pulled to national leadership development and global mentoring," he tells his wife Renee.

As the months roll on, Pastor James begins to sense somewhat of a condescending tone from the young man. Jimmy debates his instructions and makes sure to point out his oversights or misstatements. He feels like Pastor James is out of touch with the culture and even makes fun of his wardrobe.

"You are old school, Pastor James…perhaps it's time to step aside and let us take this to the next level," he says one day. Pastor James soon realizes that he is being shadowed by a disrespectful conduit—a Parasite!

"A silly daughter teaches her mother how to bear children," says an Ethiopian proverb. Think about the wisdom in that proverb. Can any sensible daughter even think she can really assume such a position?

A former mentor of mine used to say, "Never allow the invitation to intimacy to be destroyed by the contempt of familiarity." In other words, one must be careful not to let familiarity destroy intimacy. Depending on the depth of relationship, Conduits have access to the private lives of their Coaches. Even then, the access must never be abused. They must respect the Coach's private space, personal time, and boundaries, no matter how much access they think or feel they have. Remember, Coaches are not buddies or pals. To the Conduit, they are not Cheerleaders; and it's irresponsible and foolish to try to turn one's Coach into a Cheerleader.

The Bible advises:

> …And when you find a friend, don't outwear your welcome; show up at all hours and he'll soon get fed up (Proverbs 25:17 TM).

A Wise Conduit Never Attempts
to Turn His Coach Into a Cheerleader.

Wise Conduits know that it is impossible to replicate the life of someone they don't respect.

#5: A Winning Attitude

I remember mentoring a young man who expected me to call and talk with him every free second I had. He would pout and throw fits if a day went by without hearing from me. He was needy, and what began as an exciting formative journey quickly turned into a co-dependent relationship. Like a Parasite, he drained and exhausted me; before long, I started to avoid his calls. That relationship did not last long.

People with winning attitudes look at the long-term benefits of growing and learning from their Coaches. They realize that their attitudes determine the outcome of every situation. If you have a winning attitude, you will see the positive side of issues, problems, and circumstances. Having a winning attitude considers and treats others with respect. Growing and maturing comes naturally for those who have a good attitude about themselves and life.

One of the most frustrating things for Coaches is to pour into someone whom they have to constantly prop up to grow. It's the responsibility of the Conduit, not the Coach to pursue the relationship, even though they both desire the same outcome—reproduction and maturity!

HIGH-MAINTENANCE, ROLLER COASTER, UP-AND-DOWN
COUCHING RELATIONSHIPS BECOME PARASITIC.

#6: Growth Potential

True Conduits show potential for growth. This motivates the Coach to keep sowing seeds of encouragement and support into their lives.

Coaches want their Conduits to ask questions and keep their interest in them. One thing I have learned through the years: *my desire for the growth and development of those I coach should not exceed their own.* In other words, inasmuch as I desire success and fulfillment for my Conduits, protégés, or spiritual sons, I cannot want it more than they do. They have to burn with the passion to become. They must keep their own lamps burning; otherwise, they are in danger of becoming Parasites. Flattering as it might be to have someone shadow me for years, they must sooner or later jump out of the chute. Conduits must grow wings and become. Sooner or later, the echo must find its voice. Eventually, the student must become a teacher.

EVENTUALLY THE ECHO MUST FIND ITS VOICE.

Jesus said:

> ...*much is required from those to whom much is given, and much more is required from those to whom much more is given* (Luke 12:48).

And when the Conduit has reached a certain level of maturity, he is now ready to coach. He has been blessed with success and fulfillment. He has the responsibility to reach back and take the hand of a young protégé, an apprentice, a disciple, and a life-student—a Conduit! To him, knowledge, wisdom, experience, and other rich resources have been given, and indeed much more is required of him to pass it on to someone else. It is now his turn to carry the baton and coach another. An Ethiopian proverb says, "He who learns, teaches."

CHAPTER PRINCIPLES

1. Conduits are life students dedicated to sitting at the feet of seasoned coaches.

2. Everyone has a Goliath.

3. Blind spots are inconspicuous to the one who has them.

4. Knowledge without application leads to frustration.

5. God will often assign people to lend us a hand and thus save us years of mistakes and foolishness.

6. Walking into your destiny will often call for you to learn from God through others.

7. Conduits attach to grow, Parasites attach to drain.

8. True Conduits are open books.

9. A godly Conduit is a pleasure to instruct.

10. A wise Conduit never attempts to turn his Coach into a Cheerleader.

11. High-maintenance, roller coaster, up-and-down coaching relationships become parasitic.

12. Eventually the echo must find its voice.

Chapter Seven

THE COACH

Older than you by a day, more knowledgeable than you by a year.
—Arab Proverb

Let's now discuss the second kind of vertical relationship—the Coach!

You might call them influencers, teachers, instructors, fathers, dream releasers, or life coaches, but I prefer to call them Coaches. Very few people ever attain greatness without them. Coaches are vastly different from Cheerleaders. While Cheerleaders celebrate your past accomplishments, Coaches anticipate your future performance.

WHILE CHEERLEADERS CELEBRATE YOUR PAST ACCOMPLISHMENTS, COACHES ANTICIPATE YOUR FUTURE PERFORMANCE.

Coaches are people who love you too much to leave you the way you are. They appreciate your past, but see untapped potential within you. They are convinced that you can become more than what you are. They belong in your future. In order to make effective strides toward your tomorrow, you must invest time in Coaches. Eleventh century scholar Sa'di Gulistan said, "Court the society of a superior, and make much of the opportunity, for in the company of an equal thy good fortune must decline."

Coaching is an exchange between a Coach and a Conduit in order to facilitate the growth and improvement of the latter. Whether it's learning how to pray, relate to others better, become a better spouse or parent, communicate effectively, or balance priorities, coaching helps Conduits access the information and conditioning they need.

Even though the Coach might be an expert in the Conduit's area of need, he is primarily an observer, a listener, a wall on which a student of life can bounce ideas and find encouragement to become all God wants him to be. He creates an environment where the Conduit ultimately becomes self-correcting and self-motivated.

Please note that although I use the term "he," it is merely for ease of conversation. Women are excellent Coaches. My very first mentor was a woman. When I was 13 years of age, Pastor Mary Lwanga taught me how to hear God's voice and to move in the gifts of the Holy Spirit. I would not be the minister I am today without her hand upon my life. Women are experts in many fields and I urge them—as I do men—to lend themselves to becoming Coaches—encouraging others to reach for God's best in their lives.

The idea of coaching has become somewhat of a trend these days. There is a lot of talk on the subject although few people really understand the concept. For example, some Christians think coaching is the same as discipleship. Though both are modeled in Scripture, coaching is relationship-based, while discipleship is content-based. The focus of a Coach is the Conduit and his or her agenda, whereas discipleship is all about the discipler's spiritual agenda.

Proverbs says:

> *Give yourselves to disciplined instruction; open your ears to tested knowledge* (Proverbs 23:12 TM).

In other words, plant your life in a relationship that will instruct your life.

SUCCESSFUL PEOPLE FIND AND ENLIST THOSE WHO ARE PROVEN WINNERS IN THEIR FIELD OF PURSUIT.

Conduits embrace people with proven wisdom whose achievements exceed their own and model the growth they desire. Dr. William Greenman makes a startling statement. He writes, "Success is guaranteed when you enlist wise counsel. It is proportional to the quality of people with whom you surround yourself."[1]

No matter who you are, you will reach a point on your journey where you could use a helping hand or godly instruction to help you navigate through different situations and seasons. Let's discuss a few of those instances.

PIVOTAL DECISIONS

We need Coaches when making pivotal decisions. There are certain decisions that have potential to greatly and permanently impact your life. It might be a marriage decision, a career change, or a decision to start a family. In such cases, a Coach will help you muddle through the different options and emotions in order to reach a decision that will propel you toward your goals.

Remember this: you need someone who can look at your life from the outside. You need someone who will not beat around the bush, but will tell you what you need to hear, not necessarily what you want to hear. You need "disciplined instruction," as Proverbs 23:12 puts it. Let's read that verse again.

> *Give yourselves to **disciplined instruction**; open your ears to **tested knowledge**.*

There have been times when I thought I was hearing from God. Boy was I ready to run with my convictions! Thank God for Coaches, who helped bring biblical and directional balance to my life. They provided principle-driven counsel that helped me make pivotal decisions that were not emotionally driven.

BETTER TO GET PRINCIPLE-DRIVEN COUNSEL
THAN EMOTION-BASED OPINIONS.

TURNING POINTS

Another reason we need Coaches is to help us negotiate life's turning points. Life is interjected by seasons, and on our journey we experience many unexpected turning points. These may include career adjustments, educational opportunities, parenting, marriage, remarriage, midlife developmental changes, job retirement, and so on.

You will benefit greatly if you have a Coach who is willing to take your hand and help you negotiate life's turning points. This is why the Bible calls it "tested knowledge." Tested knowledge is not theoretical pontification, but life lessons that are often evidenced with scars. The French have a proverb that says, "It's in old kettles that one makes the best soup."

A Seasoned Coach Is a Living Witness to the Folly or Wisdom in a Decision.

God's Word says:

> *Just ask the former generation. Pay attention to the **experience of our ancestors*** (Job 8:8).

As we already discussed, experience can indeed be an effective teacher, but only when studied and carefully evaluated. Experience in and of itself does no one any good. Our ancestors or predecessors have done most of what we are going to do. They have experienced what works and what doesn't. They wish they could hit the rewind or reset button and undo some of the stupid decisions they made. Unfortunately, that is not possible. What is possible is what the Bible says: we would be wise to listen to our ancestors and learn from their mistakes and successes.

TRAGEDY

Jesus said:

> *...In this world, ye shall have tribulation: but be of good cheer; I have overcome the world* (John 16:33 KJV).

The word "tribulation" is the Greek word *thlipsis*, which describes "stressful circumstances or extreme pressure." It can mean "distress, affliction, or trouble." Thlipsis, like death in the family, catastrophes, financial hardships, divorce, and other traumatic moments are mostly unavoidable. Many are part of life's journey. In such situations, the company of a godly Coach will prove invaluable. When you suffer one of life's harsh blows, a

Coach will cry with you, and help you heal so you can get up and continue to pursue your dreams. By watching others who emerged victoriously from similar circumstances, we can learn that one defeat does not necessarily mean we lose the war. God does indeed wipe away tears, and gradually by His grace bitter tears can be turned into joy.

I love the New Living Translation of the same verse. It reads:

> *I've told you all this so that trusting me, you will be unshakable and assured, deeply at peace. In this godless world you will continue to experience difficulties. But take heart! I've conquered the world.*

Coaches Show Us That One Blow
Does Not Necessarily Mean a Final Blow.

The Bible also says that:

> *...Weeping may endure for a night, but joy comes with the morning* (Psalm 30:5).

FAILURE

No matter how big your dream, how positive your attitude, how wonderful an inner circle of friends you have, or how much you focus your energies on following your vision, you will at some point or other encounter setbacks. The problem is that most of us completely lose focus when we experience failure. We miss the big picture and abort our dream. Says H. Stanley Judd, "Don't waste energy trying to cover up failure. Learn from your failures and go on to the next challenge. It's okay to fail. If you're not failing, you're not growing."[2]

James says:

> *Consider it **a sheer gift**, friends, when tests and challenges come at you from all sides. You know that under pressure, your faith-life is forced into the open and shows its true colors. So don't try to get out of anything prematurely. Let it do its work so you become mature and well-developed, not deficient in any way* (James 1:3 TM).

As a teenager, I always felt surrounded by failure—at school, at home—everywhere! I remember my mother waking me up in the wee hours of the morning to buy groceries. In order to get a good shot at buying these highly rationed essential commodities like sugar, salt, soap, and cooking oil, I had to get a good spot in the queue at the local grocery store as early as I could. I dreaded those long five-hour lines.

All this, coupled with the political anarchy and an unstable family environment, created the impression in my mind that I was doomed to a life of hopelessness and lack—a life of failure!

Even after I accepted Christ into my life, I battled self-pity. "Why was I born here with all this poverty and hunger? Why do I have to duck bullets and jump over my friends' dead bodies? Why me?" I often moaned and complained.

Thank God He brought a mentor to help me. During my turbulent teen years, my pastor, John Kibuuka, took special interest in my future. He encouraged me and guided me through one of the most trying times of my life. He helped me make sense of my broken family and strained personal life. Thank you, Pastor John!

The Bible says:

> *Refuse good advice and watch your plans fail; take good counsel and watch them succeed* (Proverbs 15:22 TM).

The Amplified Bible version of Proverbs 15:22 says:

> *Where there is no counsel, purposes are frustrated, but with many counselors they are accomplished.*

WHILE IT'S STILL NIGHT, LOOK FOR A COACH
WHO HAS TASTED THE JOY OF MORNING.

An Ivorian proverb states, *"The death of an elderly man is like a burning library."*

When God began to teach me about this subject of Coaches, I was very excited. I began looking for Coaches—for men and women who had gone before me. I enlisted Coaches in all the major areas of my life. To my disappointment, I soon discovered that just because some of these great men and women had achieved tremendous successes, not every one of them could help me. In other words, merely being successful or having great accomplishments is not enough.

Being Successful Doesn't Always Make a Good Coach.

Through prayer and much study, the Holy Spirit began to teach me concerning qualifications of a godly Coach. I wrote down several things I needed to see before inviting someone to speak into my life. God used my keenness to uncover many a controller and a manipulator.

Over the years, I have discovered that the following seven qualifications of a true, godly Coach should be considered when deciding who you should ask to be your Coach.

#1 True Coaches Are Honest

I remember one of my Coaches confessing to me that he had been holding back correction because he didn't want to offend me. "Dennis, I really respect you and don't want to upset you," he said. "Pastor," I replied, "Just tell me the truth. I might cry after you are done with me, but I will pick myself up and do what I need to do."

True Coaches must be honest. They do not hold back counsel, correction, or help because they don't want to hurt your feelings. They are assigned to you to sharpen you and tell you what you need to hear—not what you want to hear. Whereas your friends basically love you the way you are, a true Coach loves you too much to leave you the way you are.

Coaches Are Not Cheerleaders.

A Cheerleader celebrates you and is in your life to make you feel great about your accomplishments and what you are. A Coach, on the other hand, often doesn't even care too much about your achievements or what you have done. He is more concerned about your future and what you can become. Someone who cannot be totally honest with you cannot coach you.

I remember winning a major championship soccer tournament in high school. We rushed into the changing rooms expecting pats on the back from our coach. He had pushed us so hard and we'd done it! His words? "Good execution, kids. Now get some rest, and I will see you here bright and early Saturday morning. Remember, we now have a regional championship to win." I was bothered. "'Good execution'? Is that all he had to say? Man, we worked so hard to win this cup," I complained. I wanted my coach to act as a cheerleader. I had yet to learn that his job was not to celebrate my accomplishments, but to encourage my potential.

#2: True Coaches Are Models

While serving on a board of one of the largest church denominations in the world, a friend of mine witnessed an unfair attack on a younger member of the organization. After an unsuccessful attempt to defend the brother, he took a good look around the room. Present were some of the men he had admired and respected for their accomplishments throughout the years. He had been with the organization for over 20 years. In many ways, he had looked up to them and modeled some aspects of his ministry after theirs. He had begun to enjoy some recognition and was moving up in the leadership ranks of this global ministry. He said to the young man, "Take a look around you, buddy. This is your future. In a few years, you will be just like many of these guys—bitter, vindictive, cynical, and angry. Are you sure this is what you want?" He decided it was time to quit.

A godly Coach is someone after whom you can model your life. But before you even enlist them, the question must be asked: "Has this person really done what I believe or think he or she has done? Is his or her track record genuine and legitimate?" Sometimes our perceptions aren't accurate. I remember being so disappointed after coming around some of the great ministries I had read or heard about. In reality, some of these people were just great puppeteers, orators, and marketers. They really didn't have a heart after God. Their prayer lives were miserable. Some had not picked up a Bible to read for personal growth for years, even decades—but they had large ministries and growing churches. Indeed, they looked successful in the world's eyes, but did God call them successful?

After you settle the question of legitimacy, ask, "Is this someone I would like to become?" The bottom line: if you don't admire someone, he or she cannot coach you...period! The Conduit will always ask, "What would my Coach do right now?"

You Cannot Model the Accomplishments of Someone You Despise.

I find it humorous when I read of financial gurus filing for bankruptcy. These people make a living advising people about what to do with their money, and yet cannot effectively manage their own. What duplicity! Can failure model success? Can a divorced man and woman effectively mentor a courting couple? I believe that whereas we might be able to teach or communicate knowledge generated from experience, we can only reproduce who we are.

#3: True Coaches Are Committed

I am a dreamer, with huge visions and goals for my life. My Coaches are men who are committed to helping me reach my potential and achieve those dreams. They help me put things in perspective. Sometimes they need to slow me down and at other times, they stretch me. One thing they never ever do is kill my dream. In fact, the agenda for our relationship is my dream—my destiny—and their assignment is to help me walk it out.

I must not be a burden to them because my growth is their pride and joy. In other words, they are assigned to me by God to help me. They never make me feel unwelcome. Am I going to stumble along the way? Sure. Will I let them down? Most probably. But they are committed to me. Seeing and knowing that encourages me to push through and become!

Your godly Coach believes in your potential. They are like a strong wind beneath your wings, encouraging you and spurring you on to soar, settling for nothing but the best. Once again, they are not Cheerleaders, but Coaches.

Coaches See the Untapped Potential in a Conduit; They Are Attentive to His Ultimate Future.

Coaches see in you what you yourself often cannot see. They see untapped potential and are committed to helping you push through the thresholds of change to fulfill it.

#4: Coaches Are Transparent

A few years ago, I invited a successful millionaire-businessman to coach me in the area of my finances. Although he transferred valuable knowledge in some areas of financial stewardship, our relationship did not grow into its full potential. He was vague and impersonal. He never talked about his mistakes or shortcomings. As far as he was concerned, everything he had done was perfect. Eventually, the Lord revealed his hidden motives to control and manipulate me, and his lack of transparency told the whole story.

Your Coach must be transparent with you concerning the struggles of the journey you have embarked upon. They must be willing to tell you where they failed or the hardships they experienced along the way, without necessarily getting overly personal.

Good Coaches Are Transparent.

One of the first questions I ask when enlisting a Coach is, "If you were to have another run at this, what would you do differently?" Talking about his or her regrets and mistakes helps me know what to avoid or prepare for. One thing is for sure…my Coaches are human just like me, so I am not disappointed when I see their weaknesses. On the contrary, I am encouraged and know that if they made it in spite of the mistakes, I can too!

#5: Coaches Are Teachers

Unless Coaches can transfer the knowledge gained from their journey, that coach is really not beneficial to you. A basic characteristic of good Coaches is that they are able instructors or teachers. They can articulate the lessons gleaned from their life experiences.

Not every coach uses the same coaching style. We shall look at this area in the next chapter, Coaching Dynamics. Some Coaches prefer not to lay out or even discuss their agenda. Like Elijah, they want the Conduit to follow and glean on the fly. They are spontaneous. But regardless of the coaching style, true Coaches have to be able to transmit the life lessons needed to catapult their Conduits to their God-given destinies.

My Coaches are teachers, even though not in the conventional, classroom way. They are able to show me their scars and articulate the stories behind them, and why they have them. They take great care and adequate time to interpret what the wrinkles upon their faces mean. They are teachers!

#6: Coaches Celebrate You

I once had a great leader that I really admired. This guy was a huge achiever who personified everything I wanted to be. After months of pursuit, I was elated when he accepted my invitation to a monthly sit-down lunch.

But after three months of three-hour-long lunches, I was frustrated. What promised to be precious moments in the School of Instruction had become self-aggrandizing oratories of the achiever's accomplishments. For hours, the egotistical guru went on and on about his successes and conquests. He never affirmed me even once. Although I was not looking for him to be my Cheerleader, I still needed encouragement and perhaps an occasional pat on the back, or a "well done, son." It was all about him, his circle of superstar buddies, and mega ministry.

Eventually, I dissolved the relationship. I figured that if I wanted a list of accolades, I could easily find those online or in any one of his recent books. What I wanted was a godly mentor to take my hand and guide me through the rigorous terrain of my early ministry years.

EGOCENTRIC, SELF-ABSORBED,
KNOW-IT-ALLS DON'T MAKE GOOD COACHES.

Remember that a Coach's primary assignment is to see you released into your assignment. The relationship is built around *your* dream or agenda, not theirs; and as such they ought to be able to stop and recognize your progress when you make noticeable strides or work through obstacles.

#7: Coaches Are Learners

A Congolese proverb says, "No matter how full the river, it still wants to grow." Good Coaches must be teachable. No matter how knowledgeable, accomplished, or experienced they might be, no Coach is perfect and beyond learning. Renowned author and philosopher-poet Ralph Waldo Emerson said, "Every man is superior in some way; in that I can learn from him."[3]

My Coaches are teachable and that encourages me to learn from them. Having served in over 60 nations at the time of this writing, I have been humbled to teach some of my Coaches a lot of things about culture and the intricacies of cross-cultural ministry. In many ways, I am encouraged to see that they are open to new information and personal growth.

GOOD COACHES ARE TEACHABLE.

Think about a banana. As long as it's green, it's growing. The moment it ripens, it begins its end. The Bible says:

> See that man who thinks he's so smart? You can expect far more from a fool than from him (Proverbs 26:12 TM).

On my journey, I have seen huge ministries destroyed solely because they had no Coaches. They wanted to do it all in their own way, on their own terms, in their own time, by themselves—alone! Some even said they were too big for counsel. Admitted President Woodrow Wilson, "I not only use all the brains I have, but all I can borrow." Solomon advises:

> People who despise advice will find themselves in trouble; those who respect it will succeed. Get all the advice and instruction you can, and be wise the rest of your life (Proverbs 13:13, 19:20).

Writes Dr. Rick Renner:

> It is extremely tragic, but many believers are too proud or too frightened to open their lives up to another believer and receive godly counsel and prayer—and just plain friendship... they would rather be miserable and tormented than have anyone know about them.[4]

Proverbs 18:1 in the New King James Version says:

> A man who isolates himself seeks his own desire; he rages against all wise judgment.

ENDNOTES

1. William D. Greenman, *Discover Your Purpose, Design Your Destiny, Direct Your Achievement* (Shippensburg, PA: Destiny Image, 1998).

2. John C. Maxwell, *Failing Forward* (Nashville, TN: Thomas Nelson, Inc., 2000), 50.

3. http://www.heartquotes.net/Emerson.html; accessed 3/4/10.

4. Rick Renner, *Dream Thieves* (Tulsa, OK: Albury Publishing, 1992), 113.

CHAPTER PRINCIPLES

1. While cheerleaders celebrate your past accomplishments, coaches anticipate your future performance.

2. Successful people find and enlist those who are proven winners in their field of pursuit.

3. Better to get principle-driven counsel than emotion-based opinions.

4. A seasoned coach is a living witness to the folly or wisdom in a decision.

5. Coaches show us that one blow does not necessarily mean final blow.

6. While it's still night, look for a Coach who has tasted the joy of morning.

7. Being successful doesn't always make a good Coach.

8. Coaches are not Cheerleaders.

9. You cannot model the accomplishments of someone you despise.

10. Coaches see the untapped potential in a Conduit; they are attentive to his ultimate future.

11. Good Coaches are transparent.

12. Egocentric, self-absorbed know-it-alls don't make good Coaches.

13. Good Coaches are teachable.

Chapter Eight

COACHING DYNAMICS

You do not teach the paths of the forest to an old gorilla.
–Congo Proverb

*Learning is acquired by reading books; but the more necessary
learning, the knowledge of the world, is only to be acquired
by reading men, and studying all the various editions of them.*
–Lord Chesterfield

I remember when a young man I had led to Christ asked me to actively disciple him. I panicked. I did not feel ready for such responsibility. Questions flooded my mind, such as:

1. What if I don't have what it takes?

2. What if I give him the wrong advice?

3. What if I cannot answer his questions?

4. What if he rejects my advice?

5. What if he eventually rejects me?

6. What if he realizes he really doesn't need me?

7. What if I cannot find the adequate time to do this?

8. How and where do I even begin to do this?

Although I was scared, I accepted his invitation, and thank God I did, because today, he is a powerful minister of the Gospel of Jesus Christ.

Over the years, I have been discipled and coached by many a godly man or woman. I have noticed that each one had his preferred style of coaching. Some preferred structure, while others like spontaneity, hence the terms, Structured Coaching and Spontaneous Coaching.

THE STRUCTURED COACH

The Structured Coach takes a decidedly cautious approach to mentoring. He believes in making sure that all bases are covered before he even commits to the journey. One Structured Coach I had took me through numerous loops and strident qualifications before he committed to the relationship. However, once he did, I had his full commitment. He was all in! He never once canceled an appointment or failed to come through on a promise. It was awesome! And when he felt that his assignment was done, he gracefully ended our coaching relationship.

Structured Coaches are not quick to reveal or announce their scars. They generally prefer private one-on-one coaching to overt in-your-face open instruction. They are careful about their methods. Whenever I sit at the feet of a Structured Coach, I had better have a notepad handy. They don't like to be misunderstood or even misquoted because of their keen attention to detail. They take their role very seriously. They like to assign research projects and personal assessment exercises. They are detail-oriented and plan well ahead. They get concerned when a Conduit doesn't ask questions.

There are two main dangers that I have noticed with this coaching method.

I. Clones

Because Structured Coaches tend to rigidly enforce their methods or techniques, they often neglect the fact that they are in their Conduits' life as pointers not production specialists. They sometimes forget that people are not projects, but individuals rich with shades of complexity. The psalmist writes:

Thank you for making me so wonderfully complex! Your work-manship is marvelous—and how well I know it (Psalm 139:14).

WE ARE ALL UNIQUE, WITH UNIQUE GIFTINGS AND CALLINGS.

Paul writes in Romans 12:2 that:

Just as our bodies have many parts and each part has a special function, so it is with Christ's body. We are all parts of His one body, and each of us has different work to do. And since we are all one body in Christ, we belong to each other, and each of us needs all the others.

This means that although we need people to pour into our lives and to guide us as we grow, every one of us is unique and has a distinctive function or role to play. No two of us are the same. Both the hand and the leg are important to the body's overall function. One can never be the other, but both are unique and different. Our significance is hidden within our difference from those around us, not similarities. The Lord told Jeremiah:

Before I shaped you in the womb, I knew all about you. Before you saw the light of day, I had holy plans for you: A prophet to the nations—that's what I had in mind for you… I know what I'm doing. I have it all planned out—plans to take care of you, not abandon you, plans to give you the future you hope for (Jeremiah 1:5; 29:11 TM).

Structured Coaches need to keep in mind that although Conduits need them, they can only instruct, model, and be examples to them. God made each of His children unique—He isn't interested in clones. Inside of each one of us is divine destiny, holy plans—God's dream!

ONLY GOD CAN BRING OUT THE UNIQUE PURPOSES FOR WHICH HE DESIGNED US.

---

2. Control

The whole concept of coaching is to enable the Conduit to grasp vital life lessons that will enable him or her to make independent decisions and to take responsibility for executing God's mandate for his or her life. Ideally, when people are ready to fly, they ought to be released and supported. Will they make mistakes? Of course they will! But that, unfortunately, is part of the process. Regardless of the Coach's training or mentoring skills, his or her Conduits will stumble, but as the Portuguese say, "Stumbling is not falling."

EVENTUALLY THE CONDUIT MUST FIND HIS LANE,
GET IN HIS LANE, AND STAY IN HIS LANE.

Structured Coaches tend to vicariously live through their Conduits. Like any good Coach, they cannot bear to see them make the same mistakes that they made. Thus they hold on to them, and sometimes never see them through to independence. Like a father who refuses to let his child grow to independence from him, sooner or later, frustration turns to resentment and even rebellion.

I have been blessed to have some great relationships with some of the world's greatest emerging church leaders. It is saddening to hear almost the same story from most of them: "Man, I loved my spiritual father. Without him, I would not be here. Unfortunately, he has totally cut me off; won't even talk to me. Why? Because I left his house! Inasmuch as I cherished his influence in my life, it was time to go—to grow and leave the proverbial nest, but he took that as rejection and rebellion. He calls me an Absalom."

THE SPONTANEOUS COACH

Spontaneous Coaches believe that real impartation is not formulaic; it does not happen by some preset methodology. They believe that it is caught, not taught. It's unrestrained and uninhibited.

Spontaneous Coaching considers the fact that we are all different and varied in our personalities and character. What works for one Conduit, might not work for another, which is often true. One of my Spontaneous Coaches likes to say, "Dennis, the Holy Spirit works differently in the lives of His children because He has a unique design and purpose for each one of us. Besides, not everyone is at the same growth or maturity level."

Notwithstanding, spontaneous coaching also has its downsides, including the following two: inattentiveness and premature release.

1. Inattentiveness

Spontaneous Coaches tend to miss important details of needs present in their Conduits. Because they are not process-driven, they are not always aware of factors that might prevent the effective transfer of knowledge, wisdom, and impartation. Sometimes Conduits have questions that need structured responses. Sometimes, they need to develop disciplines to break bad habits with new patterns. Spontaneous Coaching doesn't readily provide that because it does not advocate boundaries and margins. Again, to this style of coaching, the transformational process happens in a continuum of change and spontaneity.

2. Premature Release

It is not uncommon for a Spontaneous Coach to suddenly invite a protégé to sit in at his company board meeting, or to abruptly hand the keys to the office to his spiritual son and say, "Son, you are in charge now. If you need anything, pray. Whatever you do, don't call me!" This can be very dangerous. I have seen ministries ruined because a Coach prematurely released too much power or responsibility to an under-conditioned or an ill-prepared Conduit.

I suppose it's always best to add both elements of structure and spontaneity into the coaching process. But regardless of their preferred method of coaching, it is expedient that the process has the following four elements within it:

1. Confidentiality

2. Time Commitment

3. Determination

4. Patience

Let's discuss these briefly.

Confidentiality

It is extremely important that there is absolute confidentiality within the coaching relationship. Sometimes Conduits will divulge personal information that would be very embarrassing if repeated. I make it a habit to assure those I coach that although my wife and I are very close and know almost everything about each other, conversations with my Conduits are confidential. Ingrid does not have the grace to handle what God has given me to do. Otherwise she would do my job. Likewise, I never get between her and those she coaches and counsels, because similarly, I know that God has not given me the same grace she has to handle those confidences.

One pastor had a terrible habit of divulging private details of conversations from his coaching sessions to his staff members. Sometimes he would make jokes and poke fun about the poor judgments of his parishioners. Eventually he lost all pastoral credibility. Although they still respected his position and enjoyed his sermons, his congregation stopped confiding in him. He became a shame to the office of a shepherd and subsequently hurt his influence, leadership, and ministry.

Time Commitment

The Bible says:

> There is an **opportune time** for everything, **a right time** for everything on earth (Ecclesiastes 3:1 KJV).

Set yourself some timelines. The coaching process will cost you the currency of time. God has blessed every one of us with 24 hours a day to live and accomplish the purpose for which He created us. What you do with that time determines how fast you reach your goals.

GOD HIMSELF USES TIME TO PREPARE
AND TRAIN US FOR HIS WORK.

I often draw from the wisdom that I have gleaned during the seasons of dryness, plowing, and plenty that I have endured and enjoyed throughout the years. God has used these times to make me the man I am today.

A closer look at the Scriptures tells me that He has been doing this from time immemorial. Here are a few examples:

- God took 80 years to prepare Moses for a 40-year ministry!

- God took 13 years to produce a remarkable prime minister of the most powerful nation on the earth from an impulsive, simplistic young man named Joseph.

- It took 14 years of preparation before a shepherd boy named David became Israel's greatest king!

- After Elijah met his successor, Elisha (see 1 Kings 19:19), he invested 10 years into his life before he was ready to not only inherit Elijah's anointing, but supersede his accomplishments (see 2 Kings 13).

- And what about the 30 years of molding before John the Baptist started his ministry?

- God took 30 years to ready Jesus for a 42-month earthly ministry.

- Finally, after Paul had his Damascus Road experience in Acts chapter 9, it took 14 years of preparation before being thrust into the thick of his assignment in Acts chapter 13.

Good coaching relationships are never hit-and-run relationships. Some personal growth experts assert that real coaching is a life-long journey. It takes time to effect change or to create real transformation. Expect to be in this for the long haul.

To the Ephesians, Paul writes:

> *Look carefully then how you walk! Live purposefully and worthily and accurately, not as the unwise and witless, but as wise (sensible, intelligent people), Making the very most of the time [buying up each opportunity], because the days are evil. Therefore do not be vague and thoughtless and foolish, but understanding and firmly grasping what the will of the Lord is* (Ephesians 5:15-17 AMP).

Determination

Not all coaching relationships work out or produce the desired end. Whether due to miscommunication, false expectation, or poor chemistry, some collapse before they even take off. Part of the problem is that most Coaches completely lose focus when they experience failure. They miss the big picture and give up on the impartation process.

WHEN YOU FAIL, GET YOURSELF UP AND HIT THE RESET BUTTON.

I heard Dr. Robert Schuller say, "Every obstacle is an opportunity and every problem hides a positive possibility." That is very true. Keep moving forward no matter what happens. King Solomon observed:

> *No matter how many times you trip them up, God-loyal people don't stay down long; soon they're up on their feet* (Proverbs 24:16a TM).

So if your first coaching relationship was a disaster, get back to your notes. What went wrong? Is there anything you could have done differently? If there is, then equip yourself for next time. Again, do keep in mind that sometimes you are not responsible for the failure. If the Conduit is unwilling or unable to mold or learn, the relationship will break down. You are not the first coach to fail. Judas Iscariot was a Conduit along with the other 11 disciples, wasn't he? I don't see Jesus blaming Himself over his failure. And what about Adam?

I remember the tedious process of encouraging our toddlers to take those first baby steps. Over and over they would fall down and even hurt themselves in their attempts to learn how to walk. But not once did my wife or I say, "OK Adam you've had your chance and blew it. Lesson over. Don't try that again." On the contrary, we encouraged each one to try again and again, until they learned not only to walk, but also to run.

Says Dave Anderson, "Failure can be the starting point of a new venture. Failure is also the mark of a success you have worked for. When a pole-vaulter finally misses in competition, it shows how far he's come. That failure becomes the starting point for his next effort, proving that failure is not final!"[1]

The issue is not whether you will experience failure or not. That is a given. Like it or not, setbacks are part of any worthwhile formative journey. The right question is, "How do I handle failure?"

Apostle James makes this powerful statement concerning trials in James 1:2 (TM), which says:

Don't try to get out of anything prematurely.

In other words, "Don't jump out of the oven before you get cooked." The process takes time.

Coaching Is Not a Microwave Process; It's a Crock-pot Experience!

Don't expect any quick fixes or overnight miracles.

A godly Coach knows that the formative process of a Conduit will take time. He is patient. And what is patience? It's the ability to endure waiting or delay without becoming annoyed, antsy, or upset. A patient individual has the ability to tolerate being hurt, provoked, or annoyed without complaint or loss of temper.

Rick Renner writes:

Patience is the ability to remain steadfast, to continue pressing on and pressing on with a calm assurance and bold confidence regardless of adversity or the length of time that has transpired, knowing that what God has promised will surely come to pass.[2]

President Abraham Lincoln said:

A man watches his pear tree day after day, impatient for the ripening of the fruit. Let him attempt to force the process, and he may spoil both the fruit and tree. But let him patiently wait, and the ripe fruit at length falls into his lap.[3]

Coaches learn to be patient; they understand that success must take its due course to be achieved properly. Patience is an attribute that every Coach must master and demonstrate in order to help Conduits birth their God-given dreams. They need to know that Conduits will fail and mess up, and fail and mess up, until they learn to walk differently.

FIND THEM!

Whether Spontaneous or Structured, I encourage you to find a godly man or woman in your line of endeavor and shadow him or her. Find a Coach who will challenge you to reach for nothing other than God's absolute best for your life and family. Why make the same mistakes that your father or mother or predecessor made? Doesn't it make sense to simply invite them for a cup of tea or coffee and ask them how they came through challenges in life—and take notes? Isn't it smarter to have them point out the potholes before you reach them? Why not listen to their recordings or read their memoirs and journals, and learn from them?

WHY NOT SIT AT THE FEET OF A COACH
INSTEAD OF WASTING IRREDEEMABLE TIME
AND ENDURING UNNECESSARY PAIN?

You and I don't have to reinvent the proverbial wheel. The Bible says:

Follow the steps of good men instead, and stay on the paths of the righteous (Proverbs 2:20).

I know many people, including some powerful men and women of God, who know how to dream and have great productivity. Although these men and women have some degree of success, they fail to grow beyond a certain level, often because they are "lone rangers." Great ministries have been destroyed and God's mighty servants have made huge blunders because they were unwilling to enlist Coaches to help them. The Bible promises:

Those who listen to instruction will prosper (Proverbs 16:20).

There are a few men and women who have made it to the top without any help. They didn't relish the lonesome adventure. Spend a few minutes with them in private and they will tell you that if they had to do it all over again, they would find and enlist Coaches! They dreaded walking alone to the top with no one to show them the ropes.

Writes Bobb Biehl:

Every time you take on a protégé, it's like picking up a handful of snow. You put her or him out in life, and you say, "Let me pack you up, start you down through life, and if you have any questions, if you get stuck up there, let me know and I will just come down and give you a little shove, and you can roll on down the hill." Twenty miles, or twenty years later, imagine the impact and influence on history![4]

Coaching is not determined by age. I know many people, myself included, who coach others much older than they are. It's not an issue of chronological age. It's a function of maturity in one area or another. For example, one of my friends and I have a really unique relationship. Although he gleans from me spiritually as his pastor, I eagerly seek his counsel in areas of business. The duality of this coaching relationship has been an incredible blessing to both of us, hence the deep friendship we enjoy.

Coaches are not perfect, nor are they omniscient. They are ordinary men and women who have journeyed before you. They have done some things well and have also made some mistakes. Ironically, it is those less-than-perfect decisions and experiences along the way that make their lives so rich with wisdom. In fact, the rougher their journey, the richer they are—and the more blessed you will be to learn from them.

ENDNOTES

1. John C. Maxwell, *Failing Forward*, (Nashville, TN: Thomas Nelson, Inc., 2000), 191.

2. Rick Renner, *Dream Thieves*, (Tulsa, OK: Albury Publishing, 1992), 82.

3. Robb Thompson, *Excellence Dictionary* (Tinley Park, IL: Family Harvest church, 2004), 86.

4. Bobb Biehl, *Mentoring* (Nashville, TN: Broadman and Holman, 1996), 19, 26.

Chapter Principles

1. We are all unique, with unique giftings and callings.

2. Only God can bring out the unique purposes for which He designed us.

3. Eventually, the Conduit must find his lane, get in his lane, and stay in his lane.

4. God Himself uses time to prepare and train us for His work.

5. When you fail, get yourself up and hit the reset button.

6. Coaching is not a microwave process; it's a crock-pot experience!

7. Why not sit at the feet of a Coach instead of wasting irredeemable time and enduring unnecessary pain?

SECTION III

Relational Healing

Jade that is not chiseled cannot become a gem.
–Chinese Proverb

Chapter Nine

STAINS OF LIFE

Even monkeys fall from trees.
—Japanese Proverb

There have been many solid scientific studies attesting to the benefits of positive relationships with others. People with good relationships:

- Are less likely to suffer from depression and related illnesses.

- Enjoy improved mental health.

- Have stronger immune systems.

- Live longer.

Conversely, when relationships go wrong, sometimes irreparable harm remains with the victims throughout their lives. This is the focus of the final section of this book—how to heal from past painful or negative relationships.

ONLY TIME REVEALS THE TRUE NATURE OF A RELATIONSHIP.

RESIDUE

It was day seven of a weeklong mission trip to Guatemala. The group had seen some awesome things that week. Through their hands and gifts,

God had touched the needy, healed the broken, and comforted the weak. Hundreds had accepted Christ as their Lord and Savior. Everyone was on a spiritual and emotional high.

As a finale, the missions pastor who was leading the trip decided to have an extended time of prayer and connection with the team. He wanted to make sure that the life lessons of the week would not be quickly forgotten.

In his gaze were three particular people, Jennifer, an attorney, Ben, the schoolteacher, and Sam, a businessman. Although it was clear that God had done a work in these peoples' lives, something was missing. *I wonder what's holding them back*, he thought.

Before he closed the meeting, he felt the Holy Spirit leading him to pray with the team concerning their relationships. "As you return home," he announced, "allow God to bring the right people into your lives. But first, let Him heal you from the wounds of old relationships."

Almost immediately, Jennifer explodes, "Pastor, all men are liars! I don't need them and don't believe I ever will." She proceeded to tell her story. Her abusive ex-husband squandered their savings and is in jail for child molestation.

Next, Ben says: "Well, Pastor, I feel really sorry for Jennifer, but my experience has taught me the opposite. I have come to believe that it is not us men with the issue, but the women. They are manipulators! They pretend to care, but really don't. It's a ploy! Everything is a game to them. I don't have any need for them. Like her, I think I want to remain single for the rest of my life." Ben's issues began when he was nine years old. He shared with the group how his mom ran away with his father's best friend; consequently, he had to raise his brother single-handedly.

Moments later, Sam protests: "Pastor, by asking us to focus on relationships, I think you risk over-emphasizing the importance of people. People do what they want anyway. Even when you sacrifice for them and love them unreservedly." The pastor remained calm. Sam continued to talk. He shared a sad story about his drug-addicted 16-year-old son who runs the local street gang and wants nothing to do with his dad.

It was clear that Jennifer, Ben, and Sam had been affected by their negative experiences with close relationships. The pastor encouraged them to allow God to heal past wounds and erase the residue from broken relationships.

BACK TO MY MANGO STORY...

As I walked back to class, hungry and frustrated, I remember the curious and rather annoying giggles of my classmates. "Pssst...," my friend Tony motioned to me. "Come here, Dennis. You might want to find something to cover yourself with. Look at your shorts. You have a yellow stain all over the front. Everyone thinks you had a bathroom accident. Did you? What happened, bro?" Boy did I feel embarrassed!

Although I had thrown away the bad mango, it had left a stain on my shorts. I longed to get up in front of the class and explain where the stain had come from, but I couldn't. Consequently, for the next three weeks, I endured a barrage of teasing before the truth made its way around to everyone. And of course not everyone believed my story. The explanation seemed too convenient to them. "Mango stain?" they chuckled. "C'mon, he's trying to cover up his little accident. We know what happened, and no one's going to tell us different."

The same can be said concerning relationships. Although some of us do eventually walk away from corrosive relationships, we retain residue of pain, rejection, fear, apprehension, and so on from them. John Maxwell says in his book, *The Power of Attitude*, "If a man has Limburger cheese on his upper lip, he thinks the whole world smells."

NEGATIVE RELATIONSHIPS LEAVE
PAINFUL FOOTPRINTS IN OUR LIVES.

UNPAID INVOICES

Marlin's first wife passed away ten years ago from breast cancer. During their marriage, they were never on the same page regarding money matters. She always questioned him and constantly second-guessed his financial decisions. Marlin is now married to a God-fearing woman, Jackie. But every time Jackie asks him to explain a large purchase on their credit card, he raises his voice and gets jumpy. Marlin has been stained!

Steven's son is going through a rebellious teenage phase. The son is very disrespectful and challenges every instruction given him. Steven runs *Young Ministers in Training*, a mentoring program for young leaders. Unfortunately, his insolent natural son has conditioned him to react suspiciously around the spiritually hungry apprentices. Every time someone asks a question, he thinks they are challenging his authority. Unbeknownst to him, Steven is living with a relationship stain.

Miriam's last employer was ruthless, oppressive, and domineering. When her boss yelled at Miriam for arriving two minutes late because of a snowstorm, she decided to quit. God has since blessed her with an amazing new job—a job she has been praying for, for the past ten years. Inasmuch as she is very grateful, she is also disturbed. She seems to over-react every time her new boss talks about observing company tardy policy. She feels judged and picked upon. Miriam has been stained by her last employer's mistreatment.

Gabriel is a successful businessman. For the past ten years, he led the building campaign for a $20 million church complex. Shortly after the grand opening, his pastor confessed to having an adulterous relationship with his secretary. In addition, the pastor was charged with tax fraud and quickly lost his ministry. Six months later, the church closed. God has since led Gabriel to a new church with a loving pastor, a man of integrity. Gabriel has jumped in with both feet, and God has quickly promoted him. He now leads the Christian businessmen's fellowship at his new church. Unfortunately, he feels uneasy every time his new pastor talks about money. Also, Gabriel watches the pastor suspiciously as he relates to the female staff. He has been stained by his history.

⤶

A couple of years back, I visited with a close friend of mine in Guatemala City, Dr. Cash Luna. Cash had just helped me through a major ministry transition. That weekend, he had invited me to minister to his 20,000-member church, and afterward to relax and fellowship together. For two days, we visited sick parishioners, watched movies, and ate some really delicious food. We had a memorable time!

As we sat talking before I retired to pack for my trip home, Cash leaned over to me and said, "Dennis, how come you are holding back. You seem reserved to me. What's wrong?" I knew what he was talking about. I explained how I was still hurting from the demise of one of the deepest relationships God had previously brought into my life. I felt like I had given tremendously into that relationship and it turned significantly sour. My family had paid a very dear price for me to grow and nurture this relationship. At the end of the day, I felt like this individual was more interested in my contribution to his life and ministry than the well-being of my family and future. I was deeply wounded.

As tears welled up in my eyes, Cash said he was not unfamiliar with my pain. He said that he too had endured years of pain from a broken relationship with someone he served and deeply cared for. His story was eerily similar to mine. Then he turned around and made a most startling statement. "Dennis, will you please not give me your unpaid invoices from that broken relationship?" Wow…what a powerful statement!

WE MUSTN'T MAKE TODAY'S GOOD PEOPLE PAY
THE PRICE OF YESTERDAY'S BAD PEOPLE.

You see, although I could not see it, I was making Cash pay for my previous broken relationship. It was not his fault that I had picked up a bad mango. Time had to work on it and indeed it was painful. But my experience had nothing to do with my relationship with Cash.

The same can be said about Marlin, Steve, Miriam, and Gabriel in the previous examples. Although natural and easy to do, they had no right to make the pleasurable relationships in their lives pay the unpaid invoices of their past painful relationships.

TWELVE UGLY STAINS

In one way or other, we have all been stained. In fact, it is impossible to walk through life without meeting people in stained pain. In other words, as long as you interact with people, you will run into good ones and bad ones. If you have ever trusted and loved, you have been hurt! Mark Twain said it best: "When you fish for love, bait with your heart, not your brain."[1] How so very true!

After we discard the bad mangos, we may carry painful, ugly stains or residue from those broken relationships. Here are 12 main stains that may be tainting your current relationships:

1. A Broken Heart

The demise of any deep relationship causes indescribable pain that can best be described as heartbreak. This woundedness may stay with us indefinitely. Singers and poets have written about this pain for centuries. It takes a tremendous amount of work for a brokenhearted person to trust again. It's a hard stain to treat.

2. Rage

I have heard people say of their friend, "Oh man, sometimes I just don't get him. Out of nowhere, the smallest thing can set him off…before you know it, he's raving mad." The person who reacts like that is probably stained. More than likely, his disproportionate response is a defensive or coping reaction to hidden fear from a past relationship.

3. A Critical Spirit

Some of us grew up with demanding, perfectionist parents or guardians. No matter how hard we tried, we couldn't please them— nothing was good enough for them. We were never good enough. Consequently, we grow up to become critical as well. A critical spirit is a hard stain to treat.

4. Guilt

"I have repented before God, but why do I still feel distant from Him?" James asked. Unbeknownst to him, James was carrying stains from his childhood. His parents were angry and bitter; they constantly criticized his performance. He always fell short of the standard. Now that he is a Christian, he struggles to receive Christ's unconditional love. He has been deeply stained. The psalmist laments:

> My guilt overwhelms me—it is a burden too heavy to bear (Psalm 38:4).

5. Shame

Jane had an abortion when she was 15 years old. Although happily married now with four lovely kids, she struggles with her past. "I feel like a hypocrite, a selfish murderer, and cannot really receive God's forgiveness," she cries. Jane carries a deep stain of shame.

6. Rejection

Rejection says, "If James rejected you, he will always reject you no matter what." Sometimes it says, "If James rejected you, so will Jim and John." At other times, it will say, "If James rejected you, no matter how well you hide it, you are a total reject." Having a healthy relationship with someone who struggles with the stain of rejection can be a tall order—it's such an ugly stain.

7. Unforgiveness

Someone likened unforgiveness to one who drinks a cup of lethal poison, and then anxiously awaits the death of their opponent. Another saying is, "Unforgiveness is like burning down your house to get rid of a rat." This is undoubtedly one of the most damaging stains that we carry.

8. Emptiness

"You know Dennis, I don't even know why I bought it. I don't really like it, but at the time, I felt this urge to get it," one millionaire confessed to me. Inside of him was a stain that created a void that nothing could fill. He was raised very poor and had to struggle for everything. Now that God has blessed him, he unconsciously over-compensates. If he can afford it, he has to get it, even if he does not really need it. He carries a stain that only God can get in there and remove.

9. Confused Sexuality

"But what if I'm gay?" Tony cried. He had been having dreams of homosexual encounters. Although he is married with two children, he is still confused. When he was 12, a priest molested him. He never told anyone about it; but now he feels as if he might have made a mistake getting married. He feels dirty and angry. James is stained.

10. Overdependence

Jenny's first husband, Peter, constantly criticized her. "You are nothing without me. Never forget that!" he often said. She has been widowed for seven years now, and feels ready to commit to a new relationship. But her confidence is completely gone. Every time she feels ready to let herself fall completely in love with her God-fearing boyfriend, whom she knows would make a perfect companion, she hears Peter's voice. "You are nothing. Do you really think he loves you?" Jenny is struggling with the stain of overdependence.

11. Low Self-Esteem

No matter how much John compliments his wife, Kirsten, on the exceptional work she has done raising their six kids, she feels inadequate. She constantly beats herself over the head about what she is not able to accomplish. Kirsten's number one influence and role model was her mother. She was a workhorse. She taught her that women belong in the kitchen and must never mention their needs. She is dealing with the stain of low self-esteem.

12. Loneliness

Bill is isolated. He is a loner who is first to arrive at the office and often last to leave. When invited to lunch by a colleague, he says, "Man, I have so much to do…no time for friends. Sorry!" Bill is an "Army brat." As a family, they moved constantly, which means that he often had to deal with the pain of detaching from relationships. Consequently, he has learned to stay attachment-free. His stain? Crowded loneliness.

IF YOU HAVE NEVER PICKED A BAD MANGO,
YOU'VE PROBABLY NEVER BEEN MANGO PICKING.

Are you dealing with any of these stains? Friend, I challenge you to take your life back and move into what God has for you. It's time to surround yourself with winning relationships with people who are not focused or controlled by their past stains. It's time to stop negative generational patterns that have affected your parents and those before you. It's time for a change.

In my book *You Have a Dream*, I write,

> You cannot move into tomorrow with unresolved yesterdays. Friend, sometimes we find ourselves lost in a forest of relationships, not because of anything we did, but because we got the wrong directions. You might have been raped by a trusted relative or betrayed by a partner. You were the victim! In relationships, you do not choose betrayal, unfaithfulness, and manipulation or backstabbing, however, you and I do have the ability to choose how we respond to the circumstances of our lives. So what if yesterday was hurtful and rough? All of us have had our yesterdays. You couldn't prevent yesterday. It happened anyway. It's how we respond to it that sets the course of our lives. Someone rightly said, "Life is 10 percent what happens to you, and 90 percent how you respond to what happens to you."[2]

The Bible says:

> *Forget about what's happened; don't keep going over old history. Behold, I will do a new thing, now it shall spring forth; shall you not know it? I will even make a road in the wilderness and rivers in the desert* (Isaiah 43:18-19 TM).

Here is a prayer I would like you to pray with me:

> *Father God, I thank You for this moment. I turn my back on my past, painful as it might have been. I ask that You heal me, dear Lord. I ask You to remove these ugly stains of yesterday's brokenness. I lay my life down before You this day. Your Word says in Mark 11:24 that we can receive whatever we ask.*
> *I believe Your Word, and therefore I know that You have heard my prayer. Now please give me the courage to boldly walk into the future You have prepared for me.*
> *In Jesus' majestic name, Amen!*

STAIN GUARD

"Well then, how do I protect myself from relational hurts and pain?" you might ask. I call this applying "stain guard." How do you go through life without carrying hurtful residue from broken relationships?

How do you stop the cycle of rejection, criticism, sexism, racism, shame, guilt, and so on, and not pass it on to those you touch and love?

Let me give you three simple keys:

1. Don't Trust People.

2. Trust Only God.

3. Love People.

Let's examine these keys in detail.

1. Don't Trust People

Yes, I know this phrase—don't trust people—might sound a bit radical or maybe even cynical, but let's read what the Bible says. Prophet Micah declared:

> Don't trust anyone—not your best friend or even your wife! (Micah 7:5)

Sounds harsh, doesn't it? Why would God be so blunt about this? It is because He knows we are broken.

STAINED PEOPLE, STAIN PEOPLE.

The facts are: broken people break people; wounded people wound people; hurting people hurt people!

Think about these few interesting questions. Do you consider yourself 100 percent dependable? Do you always respond to situations exactly like you know you should? Basically, do you completely trust you? Paul admits:

> Yes, we had the sentence of death in ourselves, that we should not trust in ourselves but in God who raises the dead (2 Corinthians 1:9).

None of us can say for a fact that we will always respond to people in the right manner. If you cannot fully trust you, why should you trust others? Do you think it's correct to expect a different standard for others than from yourself?

It is a fact that all human beings are flawed. Here is what the psalmist says:

> *It is better to trust in the Lord than to put confidence in man* (Psalm 118:8).

The New American Bible puts it this way:

> *Better to take refuge in the Lord than to put one's trust in mortals…* (Psalm 118:8).

Also from the New American Bible, the psalmist writes:

> *Put no trust in princes, in mere mortals powerless to save* (Psalm 146:3).

Trust in Fickle Human Beings
Will Always Lead to Disappointment.

Mere mortals are fickle. They change like chameleons. Very few people esteem honor and integrity, especially in this day and age. History is rife with examples of human frailty. Simply put, if we put our trust in others, we will be disappointed.

Let's take the Lord's example. The apostle John writes,

> *But Jesus didn't trust them, because He knew what people were really like* (John 2:24).

And I am sure He was not surprised when hours after shouting, "Hosanna, blessed is He who comes in the name in the Lord" (Mark 11:9) as He entered Jerusalem, most of the same folks were shouting, "Crucify Him, crucify Him!" (Mark 15:13,20). Here is the bottom line: Don't trust people. They are not trustworthy.

The New King James version of Micah 7:5 says,

> *Do not trust in a friend; do not put your confidence in a companion; guard the doors of your mouth from her who lies in your bosom.*

2. Trust Only God

Job declares:

Though He slay me, yet will I trust in Him: but I will maintain mine own ways before Him (Job 13:15 KJV).

ONLY A CONSISTENT, STEADFAST GOD
CAN BE SAFELY TRUSTED.

The Book of Psalms is full of admonitions about trusting God. Here are a few:

...put your trust in the Lord (Psalm 4:5 KJV).

And they that know thy name will put their trust in thee... (Psalm 9:10 KJV).

In the Lord put I my trust... (Psalm 11:1 KJV).

The Lord is my rock, and my fortress, and my deliverer; my God, my strength, in whom I will trust... (Psalm 18:2 KJV).

Blessed is that man that maketh the Lord his trust... (Psalm 40:4 KJV).

In God have I put my trust... (Psalm 56:11).

James the apostle wrote:

Every good gift and every perfect gift is from above, and cometh down from the Father of lights, with whom is no variableness, neither shadow of turning (James 1:17 KJV).

The Greek word for *variableness* is the word *prallage*, which means "fickleness or likely to change, especially in affections, loyalties, and preferences."

The other word in this text in James that I would like you to look at is the word *turning*—the Greek word *trope*, which means "shifting or variation." So both words give us the idea that our heavenly Father is consistent. He is not fickle, and in Him there is no hint of alteration. In other words, God is not moody or shady. He remains the same no mater what.

He is a loving, heavenly Father committed to seeing us mature in Him. He is the One in whom we are supposed to trust! He is safe to trust. The Bible says:

> *The fear of man bringeth a snare: but whoso putteth his trust in the Lord shall be safe* (Proverbs 29:25 KJV).

So here is my conclusion. The only One we can really trust is God. Humans are frail, fickle, and full of variableness. Not God. He is consistent in His love for us. He is the One we can safely trust.

3. Love People

The final step is to love people. What exactly do I mean? What is love? Paul defines it for us:

> *Love is patient and kind. Love is not jealous or boastful or proud or rude. Love does not demand its own way. Love is not irritable, and it keeps no record of when it has been wronged* (1 Corinthians 13:4-5).

Love is patient. It does not get irritated when it does not get its way. It suffers long. It waits and does not give up easily. Love is kind. It makes room for others, and it understands when they don't hit the bar. Love cares more for others than for itself. It is content and does not want what it does not have. Love does not demand its own way or insist on its own rights. It does not parade itself or display itself haughtily, as the Amplified Bible puts it. It is not self-seeking. Love is not big-headed, prideful, or boastful.

And I like The Message Bible translation of verse five. It says that love:

> *...doesn't force itself on others, isn't always "me first," doesn't fly off the handle, doesn't keep score of the sins of others* (1 Corinthians 13:5).

GOD IS LOVE.

Can you imagine how fulfilling our lives could be if we determined to genuinely love people God's way? When we can relate with others

129

through the eyes of this agape (godly) love, we enjoy the fruitfulness of real relationship. Even when others wrong us or show us their stains, we can love them through it, because we don't put our trust or confidence in them. We put our trust in God. Apostle Peter wrote:

> *Above all things have intense and unfailing love for one another, for love covers a multitude of sins [forgives and disregards the offenses of others]* (1 Peter 4:8 AMP).

With this new godly perspective, we can throw ourselves into relationships without fear of hurt. We can:

1. Be safe havens for our friends; build long-lasting friendships with our Cheerleaders; and be the godly companions they need to journey through life.

2. Nurture hungry Conduits; be to them what God desires of us; and be the tools they need to attain that propulsion toward God's best for their lives.

3. Glean from our Coaches as we safely enjoy God's guiding and loving hand to us through their earthly lives.

IF YOU LOOK AT YOUR NEW RELATIONSHIPS
THROUGH OLD LENSES, THEY ALWAYS LOOK OLD.

ENDNOTES

1. http://quotations.about.com/od/lovequotes/a/love-quotes20.htm; accessed 3/4/10.

2. Dennis D. Sempebwa, *You Have a Dream* (Peotone, IL: EWI, 2007).

———

CHAPTER PRINCIPLES

1. Only time reveals the true nature of a relationship.

2. Negative relationships leave painful footprints in our lives.

3. We mustn't make today's good people pay the price of yesterday's bad people.

4. If you have never picked a bad mango, you've probably never been mango picking.

5. Stained people stain people.

6. Trust in fickle human beings will always lead to disappointment.

7. Only a consistent, steadfast God can be safely trusted.

8. God is love.

9. If you look at your new relationships through old lenses, they always look old.

Chapter Ten

HEALING TREATMENT

Better be alone than in bad company.
—French Proverb

Suzy thought she'd finally found a real friend in Jan. She trusted her, introduced her to her family, and opened up to her in ways that she had not done with anyone else. They were bosom buddies. But after what seemed like a small disagreement, Jan decided to break her friendship with Suzy. Jan would not return Suzy's phone calls. One day, Suzy's classmate, Melissa, tells her that Jan is telling everyone that Suzy is a hypocrite. Jan is using their private conversations to slander and mar her name. Immediately, Suzy is stained.

In this chapter, we are going to discuss ways of dealing with relationship heartbreak. How do we treat stains retained after our relationships have been severed?

LOVE ONE ANOTHER

From previous chapters, the following conclusion can easily be drawn: opening yourself to relationships can cause deep pain and hurt. So what do we do? Retreat into a shell and isolate ourselves or become relationally reclusive? Build surface-only relationships that have no commitment?

Thirteen times, the Bible says we should "love one another." It also says to:

- Be kindly affectionate to **one another** (Romans 12:10).

- Prefer **one another** (Romans 12:10).

- Not judge **one another** (Romans 14:13).

- Be likeminded toward **one another** (Romans 15:5).

- Receive **one another** (Romans 15:7).

- Admonish **one another** (Romans 15:14; Colossians 3:16).

- Wait for **one another** (1 Corinthians 11:33).

- Care for **one another** (1 Corinthians 12:25).

- Carry **one another**'s burdens (Galatians 6:2).

- Serve **one another** (Galatians 5:13).

- Bear with **one another** (Ephesians 4:2; Colossians 3:13).

- Be kind to **one another** (Ephesians 4:32).

- Forgive **one another** (Ephesians 4:32).

- Submit to **one another** (Ephesians 5:21; 1 Peter 5:5).

- Not lie to **one another** (Colossians 3:9).

- Comfort **one another** (1 Thessalonians 4:18).

- Edify **one another** (1 Thessalonians 5:11).

- Exhort **one another** (Hebrews 3:13).

- Watch over **one another** (Hebrews 10:24-25).

- Not speak evil of **one another** (James 4:11).

- Not grumble against **one another** (James 5:9).

- To confess your trespasses to **one another** (James 5:16).

- Pray for **one another** (James 5:16).

- Have compassion for **one another** (1 Peter 3:8).

- Have fervent love for **one another** (1 Peter 4:8).

- Be hospitable to **one another** (1 Peter 4:9).

- Minister to **one another** (1 Peter 4:10).

- Have fellowship with **one another** (1 John 1:7).

One text that stands out to me is this one:

> *Bear ye one another's burdens, and so fulfill the law of Christ* (Galatians 6:2 KJV).

That word *burdens* is the Greek word *baros*, which means "heaviness, weight, trouble, or load." It means to stand alongside and to help carry one another's cares. And in this way, Paul writes, we shall "fulfill the law of Christ." In other words, by intimately relating as brother and sisters in Christ, we fulfill His law.

Let's look at this law again as written in the Gospel of John. It is written:

> *So now I am giving you a new commandment:* **Love each other.** *Just as I have loved you,* **you should love each other** (John 13:34).

> *I command you* **to love each other** *in the same way that I love you* (John 15:12,17).

> *I command you* **to love each other** (John 15:17).

In his personal epistle to a fellow sister in the Lord, the apostle writes,

> *And now I want to urge you, dear lady, that* **we should love one another.** *This is not a new commandment, but one we had from the beginning* (2 John 5).

Loving One Another Is a Command, Not a Suggestion.

The Bible does not say that, "I suggest you think about loving one another." Or, "It would help if you loved one another." Or, "Here is a good thing to do: Love one another." Loving one another is a *command*. It is Christ's law! And how do we obey it? By carrying one another's burdens, through building healthy relationships within Christ's family.

There are three ways that people usually handle the stains of life:

1. Ignore them.

2. Treat them.

3. Release them.

Let's look more closely at these three options.

1. Ignore Them

I remember walking home that fateful day in my yellow stained pants. What was mom going to say? How careless of me to not triple check that mango. Maybe I could have tossed it before it caused the stain. My mind began creating different scenarios. *Of course I could just pretend it's not there. I could just ignore it,* I mused.

The Easiest Way to Deal With a Stain Is to Not Deal With It.

The simplest was to deal with bad emotional residue is to pretend it's not there. But when has that ever fixed anything? Never.

When Jonathan and Paul first started hanging out, they seemed like perfect friends. Paul was very down-to-earth, caring, and fun. He did not try to dominate conversations like Jonathan's other colleagues. They enjoyed each other's company and even borrowed each other's big-boy toys. But lately Paul seems to have changed, especially since he's been hanging out with the Judson twins. Everyone at work knows them because they are popular and well-to-do. Since Paul began hanging with the Judsons, he has stopped calling Jonathan and no longer shows up to watch Monday night football like he used to. He has drifted away from the relationship.

Jonathan is the non-confrontational type. He believes that Paul knows what he's doing and eventually will come around to being the "good old Paul" that he used to be. Jonathan chooses to pray for him and keep quiet about his hurt feelings.

You Cannot Change What You Are Unwilling to Face.

The Bible says:

Don't secretly hate your neighbor. If you have something against him, get it out into the open; otherwise you are an accomplice in his guilt (Leviticus 19:17).

Instead of ignoring their relational strain, Jonathan should do something about it. The first step to any kind of internal healing is honesty. Jonathan must be brutally honest about the relationship and his feelings regarding their apparent estrangement. James writes:

For if anyone only listens to the Word without obeying it and being a doer of it, he is like a man who looks carefully at his [own] natural face in a mirror, for he thoughtfully observes himself, and then goes off and promptly forgets what he was like (James 1:23-24 AMP).

Many of us live in denial all our lives. We refuse to face our challenges or weaknesses. We don't want to confront our drawbacks, our sin, and our handicaps. We somehow imagine that we can pray it all away, or perhaps outgrow it some day! In some way, we believe that it's safer not to face our relational challenges. Admittedly, it's a lot easier for Jonathan to ignore his problem. But his denial is a surefire path to serious consequences. Have you noticed that God cannot change what you don't acknowledge? Even Socrates said, "The first key to greatness is to be in reality what we appear to be."[1]

But be ye doers of the word, and not hearers only, deceiving your own selves (James 1:22 KJV).

Stains don't fade away on their own. They must be dealt with or they will affect your life for years even after the event that caused them has long been forgotten.

2. Treat Them

After a good scolding about the stain on my pants, mother took me by the hand and led me to the woods in our backyard. "Son, take a good look at this," she said as she thrust a brown, dried leaf in front of me. "Go out there and pick as many of these leaves as you can find. Bring them to me, and I will show you how to remove that ugly stain."

Hours later, I returned with a handful of leaves. She ground them and poured the extract onto a small plate. "Here, take this and gently pour it over the stain. Rub against it until the yellow fades away. Don't be in a hurry. There now…go!" The next morning, I'd proudly parade the school halls with my stainless pair of shorts.

Jim is a very angry guy. He believes in speaking his mind no matter what. Consequently, everyone treats him with kid gloves. His son Matt avoids him like a plague because he seems to relish every moment he gets to correct him.

The other day, Jim asked Matt to clean the garage. After a full day of work, Matt is done. The garage has never been so spotless. He is proud of himself, but understandably nervous. He does not remember his father having one nice thing to say about his work—ever! Well, true to his proverbial script, Dad storms in and the first thing he says is, "Well, you never cease to amaze me, son. You seem to have this gift of negligence. It's like you need prescription eyeglasses. How on earth could you forget to dust the inner top shelf over on that back storage unit? Is this how I taught you to work? Who will ever hire you if you are so sloppy?" As Matt rushes to dust the lone shelf, he wonders, "Man, he never even looked at the new shelving system I just built for him. It will make everything so much easier to find. He did not say one word about the junk I cleaned up and how for the first time since I remember, the floor is polished. What was I thinking? Nothing I do will ever be good enough. It's just how life is."

What Matt does not know is that Jim wants to be different, but he can't. He was stained by his own father. It all started when Jim's mother died of cancer when he was only 10 years old. His father did not know how to deal with the emptiness, grief, and emotion of the loss. He started drinking heavily and often took it out on young Matt.

We all know these types of people—stained supervisors, teachers, spouses, pastors, co-workers, and so on. What do we do?

Jesus said:

> *Judge not [neither pronouncing judgment nor subjecting to cen-*
> *sure], and you will not be judged; do not condemn and pro-*
> *nounce guilty, and you will not be condemned and pronounced*
> *guilty;* **acquit and forgive and release** *(give up resentment, let*
> *it drop), and* **you will be acquitted and forgiven and released.**
> *Give, and [gifts] will be given to you; good measure, pressed*
> *down, shaken together, and running over, will they pour into*
> *[the pouch formed by] the bosom [of your robe and used as a*
> *bag].* **For with the measure you deal out** *[with the measure you*
> *use when you confer benefits on others],* **it will be measured**
> **back to you** (Luke 6:37-38 AMP).

These are some very powerful words from our Lord. Notice in verse 37, He asks us to forgive and release. He advises us to give up resentment, to let it drop, so we, in turn will be able to experience forgiveness and release. In other words, instead of focusing on fixing the stains, we must choose to look beyond them.

After teaching a relationship workshop in Kuala Lumpur, Malaysia, a woman came up to me and wanted prayer for forgiveness. She wanted God to help her forgive her former boyfriend. I was taken with curiosity since she looked 70 years of age. I thought, "How cruel of him to hurt a precious lady of this age!" As we began to pray, she stopped me and said, "I know it's been a long time, but I really need to finally put all this behind me." Even more curious, I asked, "Well, how long ago?"

"Hmmm…about 45 years ago," she answered. My heart was filled with compassion. For almost half a century, she had held on to unforgiveness and resentment. How sad that an old stain had tainted her life for so long.

I knew that Jesus heals old stains as well, so I read Luke 6:38 to her and challenged her to release her former boyfriend and let him go. She said she could not. He had hurt her, and she felt entitled to hold on to that pain. But the Holy Spirit began to convict her. For the first time, she admitted that her unforgiveness was wrong. Jesus set her free that day.

Another example of God's healing hand happened in Nashville, Tennessee. After I ministered in song with my friends Paul and Isaac, a man asked to talk to us. "For years, I have hated black people," he said. Now

I'm thinking, *Really? Have you noticed that we are black? Are you sure you want us to help you?*

He told us how 20 years before, he was beaten by a band of black kids, and they poured acid on his face, requiring costly reconstructive plastic surgery. He felt entitled to hate.

"But today I'm free. When you sang that song, 'United,' I felt God's love pouring all over me. He revealed to me how my unforgiveness was hindering His work in my life, and it was time to receive His healing. Thank you for coming. God sent you here for me!"

What an amazing testimony. Until this gentleman took the time to stop and admit his need for God to heal his stained past, he could not experience God's healing hand.

3. Release Them

Everyone likes to feel as if they "belong." C.S. Lewis calls it the Inner Ring. From his brilliant essay by the same name, he pens:

> I believe that in all men's lives at certain periods, and in many men's lives at all periods between infancy and extreme old age, one of the most dominant elements is the desire to be inside the local Ring and the terror of being left outside.
>
> Of all the passions, the passion for the Inner Ring is most skillful in making a man who is not yet a very bad man do very bad things.
>
> As long as you are governed by the desire to be in the Inner Ring, you will never get what you want. You are trying to peel an onion; if you succeed there will be nothing left. Until you conquer the fear of being an outsider, an outsider you will remain.
>
> This is surely very clear when you come to think of it. If you want to be made free of a certain circle for some wholesome reason—if, say, you want to join a musical society because you really like music—then there is a possibility of satisfaction. You may find yourself playing in a quartet and you may enjoy it. But if all you want is to be in the know, your pleasure will be short-lived. The circle cannot have from within, the charm it had from outside. By the very act of admitting you, it has lost its magic.

Once the first novelty is worn off, the members of this circle will be no more interesting than your old friends. Why should they be? You were not looking for virtue or kindness or loyalty or humor or learning or wit or any of the things that can be really enjoyed. You merely wanted to be "in." And that is a pleasure that cannot last.[2]

WE ALL HAVE A GOD-GIVEN NEED TO TOUCH AND BE TOUCHED BY OTHERS.

We recently visited a nature conservatory in Villa Hermosa, Mexico. We saw five spider monkeys indigenous to Latin America. These playful creatures have disproportionately long, spindly limbs with tiny, thumb-less hands. Because they are so agile and elusive, it's not easy to capture them. However, hunters have come up with an interesting method.

To catch spider monkeys, they use heavy containers with narrow tops and a wide bottom. In them, they put the monkey's favorite food—a Latin American nut. The hunters place these containers in the middle of the jungle and leave.

Curious, the monkeys descend from the trees to take a closer look at the hearty meal. They soon realize that they have to reach into the container to get the nuts. The monkeys reach in and grab the delicious food. Although the mouths of the containers are made small enough for the tiny thumb-less arms to reach inside the container, they are too small for a fist full with nuts to reemerge. The monkeys have a choice—to keep trying to get the nuts out or leave and go find other food. They choose the former.

For hours the monkeys struggle to get the nuts out. They won't let go of the nuts no matter what. Eventually, the hunters find them trapped by their greed and unwillingness to release what might feel good instead of safeguarding their own well-being.

When I heard this about the spider monkeys, I thought about my life. As mentioned previously, I hail from the Baganda tribe in Uganda. We are a gracious yet proud people. We absolutely hate confrontation of any kind and avoid it at all cost. We'd rather gloss over issues than face and confront them.

As I started to pursue my dream, I began to realize the necessity of changing my culturally determined perspective in this arena. "You mean culture can also be changed?" Sure it can, and often should.

Please read this startling passage with me:

> Don't become so **well-adjusted to your culture that you fit into it without even thinking**. Instead, fix your attention on God. You'll be changed from the inside out. Readily recognize what he wants from you, and quickly respond to it. Unlike the culture around you, always dragging you down to its level of immaturity, God brings the best out of you, develops well-formed maturity in you (Romans 12:2 TM).

I became aware of my need to begin to build positive relationships. Unfortunately this also meant purposely steering away from some so-called "friends" who had tagged along with me for years but whose direction was not in tandem with mine. Unwilling to offend them or cause conflict, instead of looking out for my own well-being, I backed off just like a true Muganda, choosing to hold on to them like the spider monkeys held on to the nuts until they were trapped.

Thankfully, God began to teach me how my friendships impacted my destiny. I learned that every relationship in my life was like a current moving me either toward my dream or away from it. The people who were unable to add value to my life would eventually decrease my value. This revelation began to change my life.

Worth repeating is the process I explained in Chapter 1. List all of your close associations, asking these rather brutal questions: Does this person add to me or does he or she take away from me? Does this person cheer me on or sabotage and corrupt me?

Your Associations Cause You to Either Progress or Regress.

It was a painful and difficult process for me, but my hunger for success and the burning desire to walk out my dream carried me through; the same will be true for you. If it means going without friends for a while, then so be it. A Spanish proverb says: "It is better to weep with wise men than laugh with fools."[3]

Paul writes:

Do not be deceived: "Evil company corrupts good habits" (1 Corinthians 15:33).

It is amazing how many Christians completely ignore the principle behind this verse. They continue to associate or hang out with negative people, hoping to change them in the process. Again I ask, which is easier, to pull someone up or down? Contrary to what we might think, good does not influence evil. On the contrary, almost every time, evil influences good. Let me explain further.

RELEASING PEOPLE DOES NOT MEAN WE DON'T CARE.

LETTING GO

Releasing people doesn't mean we don't love them any more. Jesus tells us to love our enemies. But the Bible does not say to walk in close fellowship with them. So in many ways, this does not have anything to do with love. We are to love all people, friends or not.

Jesus said:

If your brother wrongs you, go and show him his fault, between you and him privately. If he listens to you, you have won back your brother. But if he does not listen, take along with you one or two others, so that every word may be confirmed and upheld by the testimony of two or three witnesses. If he pays no attention to them [refusing to listen and obey], tell it to the church; and if he refuses to listen even to the church, let him be to you as a pagan and a tax collector (Matthew 18:15-17 AMP).

Jesus advises us to let wrong relationships go. If someone refuses to change, the relationship cannot remain the same. "Associate yourself with men of good quality if you esteem your own reputation; for 'tis better to be alone than in bad company," said United States President George Washington.[4]

In conclusion, we have looked at three very different ways to deal with relational stains. Let's review.

1. Ignore: Some people simply chose to ignore their stains. They pretend they are not there, and so imagine that their effects are not really prominent.

2. Treat: Others decide to face the brutality of their experiences and fight. They allow God to enable them to give, so eventually, it is given back to them, good measure, pressed down, and shaken together.

3. Release: Some choose to stop being hurt, mistreated, or maligned, saying, "I choose to trust God and release this relationship."

Friend, if you must completely dismantle your relationship circle to form a new one, then have no fear, God will help you. Your actions will not be popular, and you may face challenging times. Some of your friends won't understand, will be hurt, and will probably be angry about your decision. But you need to be confident that your choice to create a new inner ring is best—you will reach your goals and fulfill your God-given destiny by surrounding yourself with the right people. I know people who maintain wrong relationships, just because they make them feel good. How tragic!

IF YOU MUST LEAVE YOUR CURRENT INNER RING,
THEN LEAVE YOU SHOULD.

My prayer is that God will bring you wholesome relationships; that He will send you people who are:

- Loyal.

- Visionary.

- Wise.

- Stable.

- Loving.

- Faithful.

- Respectful.

- Generous.

- Godly.

ENDNOTES

1. http://edoug.org/people/morse/quotes.html; accessed 3/4/10.

2. http://www.lewissociety.org/innerring.php; accessed 2/23/10.

3. John Maxwell, *The Power of Influence* (Tulsa, OK: David C. Cook, 2001), 79.

4. Thompson, *Excellence Dictionary*, 99.

———•••••———

CHAPTER PRINCIPLES

1. Loving one another is a command, not a suggestion.

2. The easiest way to deal with a stain is to not deal with it.

3. You cannot change what you are unwilling to face.

4. We all have a God-given need to touch and be touched by others.

5. Your associations cause you to either progress or regress.

6. Releasing people does not mean we don't care.

7. If you must leave the inner ring, then leave you should.

Conclusion

Shared joy is a double joy; shared sorrow is half a sorrow.
—Swedish Proverb

As we come to the end of this book, I cannot be remiss in reminding you, dear friend, that the most important relationship any human can have is the one with God's Son, Jesus Christ. This is the starting place in your healing journey. If you don't really know Him as your Lord and Savior, you can right now. Simply pray this prayer:

> *Father God, it is written in Your Word that if I confess with my mouth that Jesus is Lord and believe in my heart that God raised Him from the dead, I shall be saved.*
> *Father, right now, I confess that Jesus is my Lord. I do believe that You raised Him from the dead. I am sorry for my sin. Please forgive me and wash me clean by Jesus' precious blood.*
> *Lord, I accept Your gift of eternal life through Your precious Son, Jesus Christ. I am a new creation. I am saved today.*
> *Now teach me to walk with You. In Jesus' name I pray.*
> *Amen.*

That's it! If you truly meant that prayer, God has forgiven you and has wiped away your sin completely, no matter how rotten or how messed up you were! God's Word says:

> *So now there is no condemnation for those who belong to Christ Jesus* (Romans 8:1).

That means that you are completely forgiven. God does not point a finger when we truly ask His forgiveness.

Take a look at this verse:

What this means is that those who become Christians become new persons. They are not the same anymore, for the old life is gone. A new life has begun! (2 Corinthians 5:17)

Now commit to reading your Bible every day and spending time with Him. Also, join a church that preaches and teaches God's Word, for there you will find other Bible-believing Christians like you who can encourage you.

Finally, believe what God says about you! You are special and He has a purpose for your life. The Bible says:

I cry out to God Most High, to God who will fulfill His purpose for me (Psalm 57:2).

⤳

I once read a story of a famous Austrian violinist named Fritz Kreisler. Many considered him the leading violin virtuosos of his day.

One day, Fritz stumbled upon a beautiful violin at an auction. He was immediately taken by the exquisite finish and sound of the instrument when he played it. But he didn't have enough cash, so he rushed out the door to get more money to buy the violin.

Upon his return, he was shocked to learn that the violin had just been sold to a collector. Words could not explain his pain. He found out where the collector lived and rushed over to try and buy it from him.

Unfortunately, the collector would not sell it. He had already picked a spot for it in his display cabinet. He agreed that the violin was indeed priceless! Finally out of frustration, Fritz begged, "May I play this exquisite violin once more before it is consigned to silence?" Reluctantly, the collector agreed.

Fritz picked up the instrument he had mastered so well and began to play. Out of the violin came a beautiful sound that moved collector to tears. "Stop, please stop," he begged Fritz. "I have no right to keep that gift of beauty to myself. The violin is yours, Mr. Kreisler. Take it into the world, and let people hear it. Its music deserves to be heard."

Friends, you and I are like that exquisite violin. We have been born with purpose. The Bible says:

> *"For I know the plans I have for you,"* says the Lord. *"They are plans for good and not for disaster, to give you a future and a hope"* (Jeremiah 29:11).

In other words, God says that He has plans for us. That word plan has a French origin. It means design or a detailed proposal for doing or achieving something. The King James Version says:

> *"For I know the thoughts that I think toward you..."* saith the Lord.

The word *thoughts* means "an idea or mental picture." Interestingly, a simple definition of the word *dream* is a vivid mental picture of where you want to go. So this verse could read, "For I know the *dream* I have for you says the Lord." Isn't that powerful?

There is music inside of us that is meant to be enjoyed by the world we touch. Life is meant to be lived. No excuses. No reservations. No holding back. God forbid that we go to our graves with it still inside of us. My prayer for you is that I die empty or vacant, having reached my full God-given potential!

Yes relationships are challenging. But if we can live by God's manual for our lives as so clearly given to us in His Word, we can enjoy the fruit of relationship.

When asked what they would do differently if they had it to do all over again, a group of elderly English people said unflinchingly, "We would risk more, worry less, and love harder." They deeply regretted all the years spent grudging, suspecting, criticizing, rejecting, and hurting from past relationships.

Friend, I encourage you to take some time and ask God to send you Coaches, Conduits, and Cheerleaders. They will immeasurably enrich your life, because like God said to Adam, *it is not good that you and I should be alone.* We need companions with whom to walk through life. We need good, solid, godly relationships with whom to share life's amazing journey.

Let me conclude with these encouraging words from the Book of Psalms,

> BLESSED (HAPPY, fortunate, prosperous, and enviable) is the man who walks and lives not in the counsel of the ungodly [following their advice, their plans and purposes], nor stands [submissive and inactive] in the path where sinners walk, nor sits down [to relax and rest] where the scornful [and the mockers] gather. But his delight and desire are in the law of the Lord, and on His law (the precepts, the instructions, the teachings of God) he habitually meditates (ponders and studies) by day and by night. And he shall be like a tree firmly planted [and tended] by the streams of water, ready to bring forth its fruit in its season; its leaf also shall not fade or wither; and everything he does shall prosper [and come to maturity] (Psalm 1:1-3 AMP).

About the Author

Ugandan-born Dennis Sempebwa has been in full-time ministry for 25 years and has served in 60 countries on six continents. He is well-known for his work as president of the legendary, award-winning gospel music group *Limit X*.

Dennis is the president and founder of *Eagle's Wings International*, a global leadership development organization, committed to empowering leaders to maximize their effectiveness. He is an author, consultant, sought-after speaker, and advisor to boards of several ministries and non-profit organizations worldwide. He holds numerous earned degrees including a doctorate in Pastoral Ministry, a PhD in Theology, and a specialized master's degree in Pastoral Counseling. He is the founder of Eagles Wings Bible Institute (USA and East Africa), an affiliate of Life Christian University, a fully accredited ministry training institution with over 140 extension campuses in 17 countries.

He pastors Sanctuary of Life Church in Chicago, Illinois. His weekly radio broadcast, "Discovering Your Purpose," is aired to millions in East Africa.

Dennis, his beloved wife, Ingrid, and their four children, Adam, Abbey, Caleb, and Judah, reside in the suburbs of Chicago, Illinois, USA.

CONTACT THE AUTHOR

Dr. Dennis D. Sempebwa
Eagle's Wings International
Website: www.eagleswingsinternaional.org
E-mail: contact@eagleswingsinternational.org

A new exciting title from
DESTINY IMAGE™ EUROPE

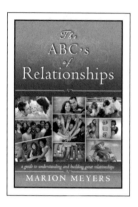

THE ABC'S OF RELATIONSHIPS
A guide to understanding and building great relationships

by Marion Meyers

Life is all about relationships—yet many of us continue to get them so wrong!

Good relationships do not come naturally, nor do they happen by accident. *The ABC's of Relationships* gives the perfect prescription for developing good, productive, and permanent relationships.

This book is an A to Z multivitamin about relationships. Every chapter touches your life in a way that makes you more emotionally and relationally whole so that you can enjoy healthier and more fulfilling connections with others.

Many things in your life are optional, but relationships are not. From the time of your conception until the time of your death, you will be involved in relationships, and the only choice you have is to build them up or tear them down.

Author Marion Meyers explains how your attitude determines how you handle life, deal with your successes and failures, and manage your relationships.

ISBN: 978-88-96727-05-8

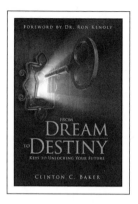

Additional copies of this book and other book
titles from DESTINY IMAGE™ EUROPE
are available at your local bookstore.

We are adding new titles every month!

To view our complete catalog online, visit us at:
www.eurodestinyimage.com

Send a request for a catalog to:

Via Acquacorrente, 6
65123 - Pescara - ITALY
Tel. +39 085 4716623 - Fax +39 085 9431270

"Changing the world, one book at a time."

Are you an author?

Do you have a "today" God-given message?

CONTACT US

We will be happy to review your manuscript
for the possibility of publication:

publisher@eurodestinyimage.com
http://www.eurodestinyimage.com/pages/AuthorsAppForm.htm